A Churchyard Diary

by Betty Mills

Published by Coast & Country Productions Ltd

A Churchyard Diary

A Churchyard Diary was first published in Great Britain in July 2009 by Coast and Country Publications, Tyldesley House, Clarence Road, Llandudno, Conwy LL30 1TW. Tel 01492-870883. www.coastandcountrymagazine.co.uk

Published, promoted & distributed by Coast and Country Productions Ltd in association with Ads2life: www.ads2life.co.uk

This paperback edition was first published in July 2009.

Red Clover

A catalogue record for this book is available from the British Library.

Paperback edition ISBN 978-1-907163-02-9

Edited by Don Hale OBE. Typeset and designed by Katie Gatton BA.

Printed and bound by Cambrian Printers, Llanbadarn Road, Aberystwyth, SY23 3TN.

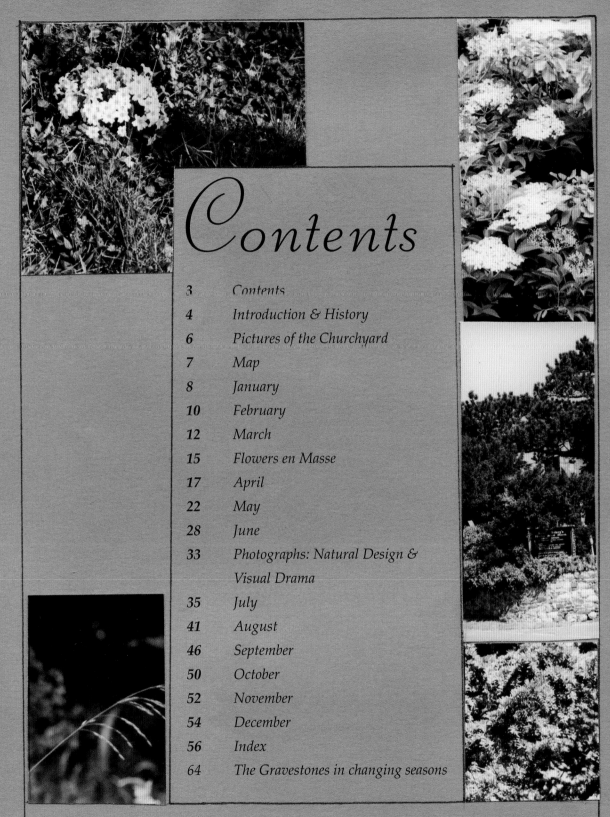

Contents

Front Cover: The South side of the Church in sunlight and shadow
21st May 1999

Back Cover: A view of the Churchyard

Page 6: Views of the Church

Introduction & History of St. Hilary's

St Hilary's Church and churchyard, about 3 acres in extent, stands on the edge of parkland attached to Gloddaeth Hall some 3 miles south of Llandudno. The entrances are from the Llandudno-Deganwy road. Beyond the churchyard, to the east, the parkland is cut through by the Llandudno Link road, connecting the town with the A55 Expressway (M6 to Holyhead).

The Lawns, Council Cemetery, is situated to the north beyond the old drive to Gloddaeth Hall (now a Public School) and the Back Car Park. Plans are currently afoot (Dec. 1999) to extend the Council property across the back of St. Hilary's Churchyard to the East.

from the park

The Lodge from which the top picture is taken is the South one by the road to Deganwy. The North one is behind the church beyond the Back Car Park.

The Mostyn Family (Lord Mostyn of Mostyn Hall - towards Fflint) who own the land around (as well as most of the land and much of the property in Llandudno) have always cared for Llanrhos. Gloddaeth Hall was one of their homes.

There is a railed, burial area in the churchyard, a sealed family vault under the South Transept of the church and several handsome, wall-mounted monuments on the walls. The present day gamekeeper cares for the parkland and the woods. The village school is leased to the Parish by the Mostyn Estate and used as the Parish Room.

Lady Augusta Mostyn who built All Saints Church, Deganwy, 1899, also master-minded the building of a hotel nearer to Llandudno (now The Links Hotel) so that the old Public House, the Queen's Head, beside St. Hilary's church, could be demolished as she thought it highly unsuitable so near to a church. (Hence the "Old Pub Area", finally added to the churchyard in 1927).

from the Link Rd.

The first church on the site was built by MAELGWYN, Prince of Gwynedd from 517-550 AD. Thought to be named for St. Hilary of Poitiers who died in 368 AD, rather than St. Eleri of Gwytherin — though no one really knows!
The church was rebuilt - in stone - in 1282 AD by the monks of Abberconwy Abbey and named, as was the custom, St. Mary's. After the dissolution of the monastries in 1535 it would have become St. Hilary's once more.
The Lytchgate is probably mid. 18th. century. The porch was added later as with the Font, pulpit, pews, stained glass windows etc. much of it in the gift of the Mostyn Family. The Parish includes Llanrhos, Deganwy, Penrhyn Bay and the Craig-y-Don area of Llandudno.

This truly magnificent bronze & marble tomb is set into the bank below the upper, mown part of the churchyard. In the church, a stained-glass window in the North Transept repeats the design - almost exactly. Both to the memory of Willam Moore Campbell 1834-1906

The churchyard, well-endowed with mature trees, prolific wild-flower growth and lovely wide views of hilly, rolling country, is a charming place. It is full of many & varied tombstones and although current efforts are being made to make all of it as tidy as the upper level, nature will still make it a lovely place to be and a powerful magnet to the wild-flower artist and photographer.

B.M. & M.J. Mills '99

Below:
The view to the South from the churchyard. The Link Rd. is beyond the post & rail fence (middle left); the new gates to Gloddaeth Hall show against the wood; Bryn Pydew is to the right & the Bodysgallen Obelisk shows further right.

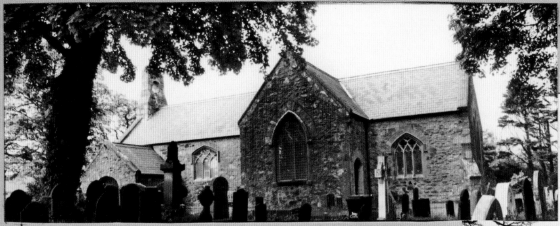

Above: the South side in MAY with the trees in full, fresh leaf.

The Church: aspects throughout the year.
The appearance of the slate-roofed, stone building
changes according to the light. Sometimes a dark,
sandy grey it turns almost golden in the summer
sun.

Below: the West end (& bell-tower) and the north side in rich,
September sun, the trees beginning to change colour.

Above: The bell-tower and West
end beyond the side-gate on
Deganwy road in MARCH. No
leaves on the Sycamores but a
carpet of Lesser Celandines on
the roadside bank.

Right: In JANUARY
the leafless trees
& the dark Yews
and Thujas frame
the church seen
from the North.
West — again from
the road but, this
time showing the
double gate to the
Old Ass Area which
lies to the north
of the mown part
of the churchyard.

6

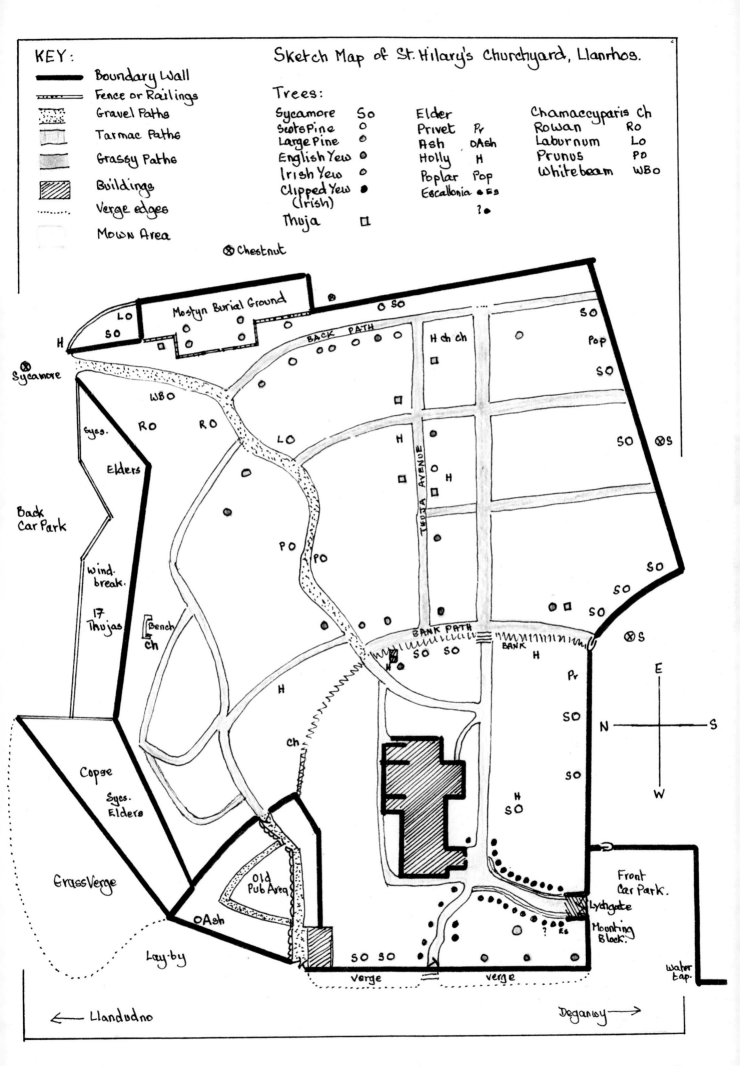

KEY:
- Boundary Wall
- Fence or Railings
- Gravel Paths
- Tarmac Paths
- Grassy Paths
- Buildings
- Verge edges
- Mown Area

Sketch Map of St. Hilary's Churchyard, Llanrhos.

Trees:
Sycamore	So	Elder		Chamaecyparis	Ch
Scots Pine		Privet	Pr	Rowan	Ro
Large Pine		Ash	OAsh	Laburnum	Lo
English Yew		Holly	H	Prunus	Po
Irish Yew		Poplar	Pop	Whitebeam	WBo
Clipped Yew (Irish)		Escallonia	Es		
Thuja		?			

⊗ Chestnut

Mostyn Burial Ground

BACK PATH

LO
SO
H
⊗ Sycamore
WBO
RO RO
Syes.
Elders
Back Car Park
LO
PO
PO
Wind. break.
17 Thujas
Bench
ch
H
ch

So
H ch ch
H
H

SO
Pop
SO

SO ⊗S

SO
SO
SO
SO

THUJA AVENUE

BANK PATH
SO SO
H
BANK
H
SO SO
Pr
⊗ S
SO
SO

ch

Copse
Syes. Elders

H
SO

Old Pub Area

Front Car Park.
Lychgate
Mounting Block.
? Es

Grass Verge

OAsh

SO SO

Lay-by

Verge   Verge

Water tap.

E
N — S
W

← Llandudno   Deganwy →

7

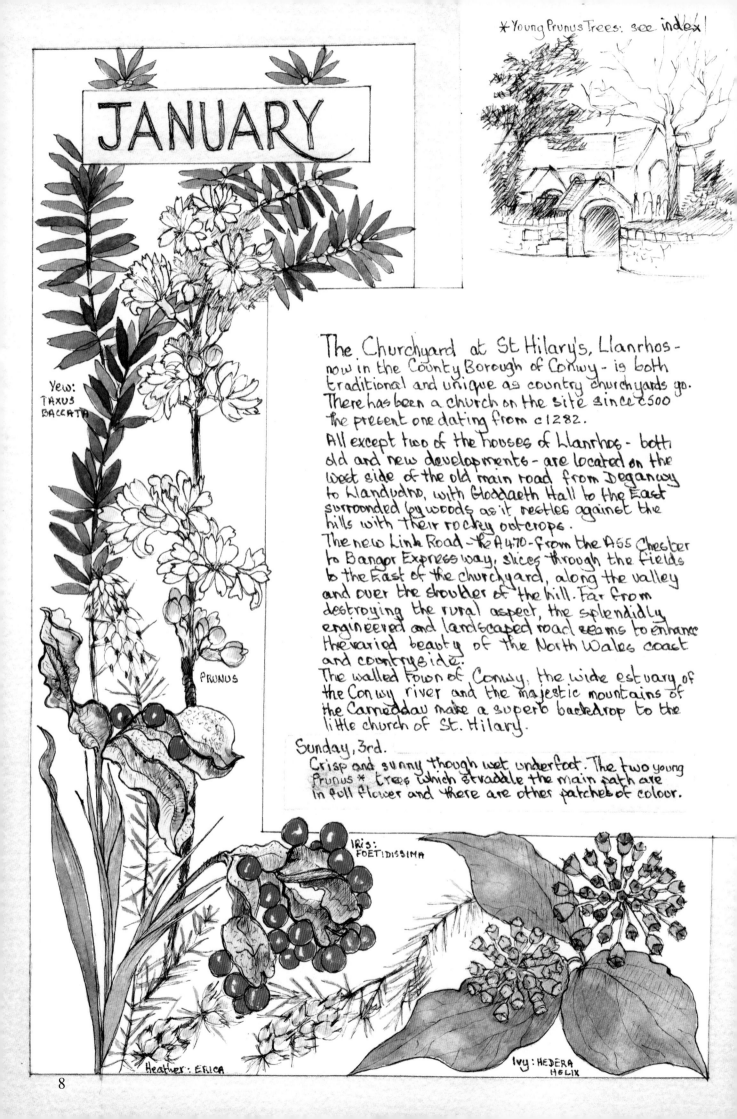

JANUARY

*Young Prunus Trees: see index!

Yew:
TAXUS
BACCATA

PRUNUS

The Churchyard at St Hilary's, Llanrhos-
now in the County Borough of Conwy - is both
traditional and unique as country churchyards go.
There has been a church on the site since c500
the present one dating from c1282.

All except two of the houses of Llanrhos - both
old and new developments - are located on the
west side of the old main road from Deganwy
to Llandudno, with Gloddaeth Hall to the East
surrounded by woods as it nestles against the
hills with their rocky outcrops.

The new Link Road - the A470 - from the A55 Chester
to Bangor Expressway, slices through the fields
to the East of the churchyard, along the valley
and over the shoulder of the hill. Far from
destroying the rural aspect, the splendidly
engineered and landscaped road seems to enhance
the varied beauty of the North Wales coast
and countryside.

The walled town of Conwy, the wide estuary of
the Conwy river and the majestic mountains of
the Carneddau make a superb backdrop to the
little church of St. Hilary.

Sunday, 3rd.
  Crisp and sunny though wet underfoot. The two young
Prunus * trees which straddle the main path are
in full flower and there are other patches of colour.

Iris:
FOETIDISSIMA

Heather: ERICA

Ivy: HEDERA
HELIX

8

January

is, by no means a barren month in the churchyard. Although most plants are "resting" and the leaves are off the deciduous trees, there is much to be seen and of interest to record:

* dead - or dried - leaves still lying on the ground since Autumn;
* new growth of mosses on walls and tombstones;
* the skeleton shapes of the many trees - all varieties of which will be recorded during the year;
* the dominating shapes and growth of the evergreen trees;
* Ivy - the upside-down plant: flowering in December and fruiting in August. (see opposite)
* Underfoot, in the grass, new leaf growth of the many plants and, in some cases, early flowers: daisies, snowdrops & primroses, amongst them.
* Some seedheads, in particular the IRIS FOETIDISSIMA (see opposite)
* Early-flowering plants in the cultivated beds alongside the paved paths: see HEATHER (opposite).

Sunday, 10th. A very beautiful day: cold + sunny after a hard frost last night. Early flowers in the grass and much new leaf growth.

Sunday, 17th. Cold and bright, rain, wind and snow over the mountains later. Fungus - fairy ring champignons - on a grave!

Sunday, 24th. Grey + raw. The first Celandines in flower

Sunday, 31st A mild, grey day: damp underfoot. The mosses on the gravestones shone brightly green in the grey light which always seems to intensify colour!

Ivy: HEDERA HELIX

Lesser Celandine: RANUNCULUS FICARIA
Fairy Ring Champignon: MIRASMI OREADES
and two varieties of moss.

Ribwort Plantain: PLANTAGO LANCEOLATA

First appearances of - on Sunday, 10th.
Daisy: BELLIS PERENNIS; Primrose: PRIMULA VULGARIS & Snowdrop: GALANTHUS NIVALIS.

New leaf growth in the grass on 10th.

Herb Robert: GERANIUM ROBERTIANUM

Alexanders: SMYRNIUM OLUSATRUM

Young Stinging Nettle: URTICA DIOICA

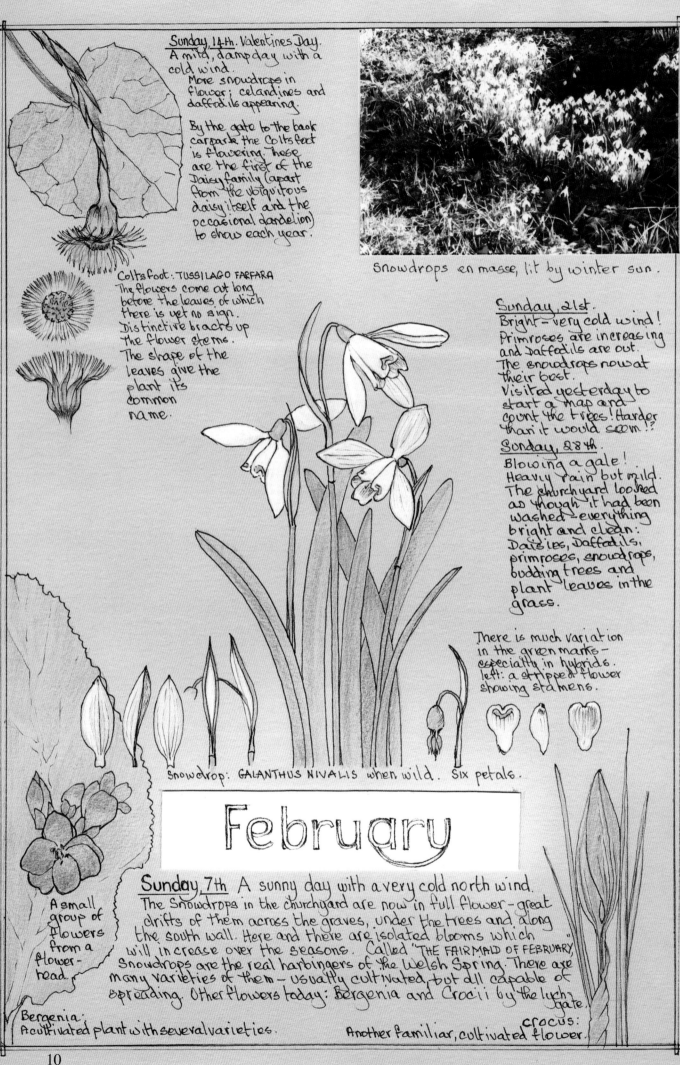

Sunday, 14th. Valentines Day.
A mild, damp day with a
cold wind.
  More snowdrops in
flower; celandines and
daffodils appearing.

  By the gate to the back
car park the Coltsfoot
is flowering. These
are the first of the
Daisy family (apart
from the ubiquitous
daisy itself and the
occasional dandelion)
to show each year.

Coltsfoot: TUSSILAGO FARFARA
The flowers come out long
before the leaves of which
there is yet no sign.
Distinctive bracts up
the flower stems.
The shape of the
leaves give the
plant its
common
name.

snowdrops en masse, lit by winter sun.

Sunday, 21st.
Bright – very cold wind!
Primroses are increasing
and Daffodils are out.
The snowdrops now at
their best.
Visited yesterday to
start a map and
count the trees! Harder
than it would seem!?

Sunday, 28th.
Blowing a gale!
Heavy rain but mild.
The churchyard looked
as though it had been
washed – everything
bright and clean:
Daisies, Daffodils,
primroses, snowdrops,
budding trees and
plant leaves in the
grass.

There is much variation
in the green marks –
especially in hybrids.
left: a stripped flower
showing stamens.

Snowdrop: GALANTHUS NIVALIS when wild. Six petals.

February

Sunday, 7th A sunny day with a very cold north wind.
The Snowdrops in the churchyard are now in full flower – great
drifts of them across the graves, under the trees and along
the south wall. Here and there are isolated blooms which
will increase over the seasons. Called "THE FAIRMAID OF FEBRUARY,"
snowdrops are the real harbingers of the Welsh Spring. There are
many varieties of them – usually cultivated, but all capable of
spreading. Other flowers today: Bergenia and Crocii by the lych
gate.

A small
group of
flowers
from a
flower-
head.

Bergenia:
A cultivated plant with several varieties.

Another familiar, cultivated flower.

Crocus:

The Evergreen Trees

Apart from some Hollies and a small number of relatively modern chamaecyparis trees, there are three main types of Evergreen tree in the walled churchyard:

Yews, TAXUS - family Taxaceae;
Pines, PINUS - family Pinaceae;
Arbor-vitae, THUJA - family Cupressaceae.

Yews two varieties: English, TAXUS BACCATA, which has a spreading habit - Irish, TAXUS BACCATA FASTIGIATA, which has a more upright habit.
9 English, 9 Irish and 27 clipped (Irish).

Pines, again two varieties:
certainly Scots Pine: PINUS SYLVESTRIS of which there are 6;
and 2 of a wider spreading variety, possibly Austrian Pine: PINUS NIGRA. More investigation of flowers and fruit should make definite identification possible.

Arbor-vitae, probably only one variety: Western Red Cedar: THUJA PLICATA. There are 6 in what is left of an avenue leading from the path below the bank to a point half-way along the back wall - plus one near an English Yew towards the south wall.

Above: the big Pine in the South-Eastern corner.
Right: the avenue of Thujas looking towards the Church.

English Yew

Irish Yew

Thuja with a magnified piece.

Pair of Pine needles.

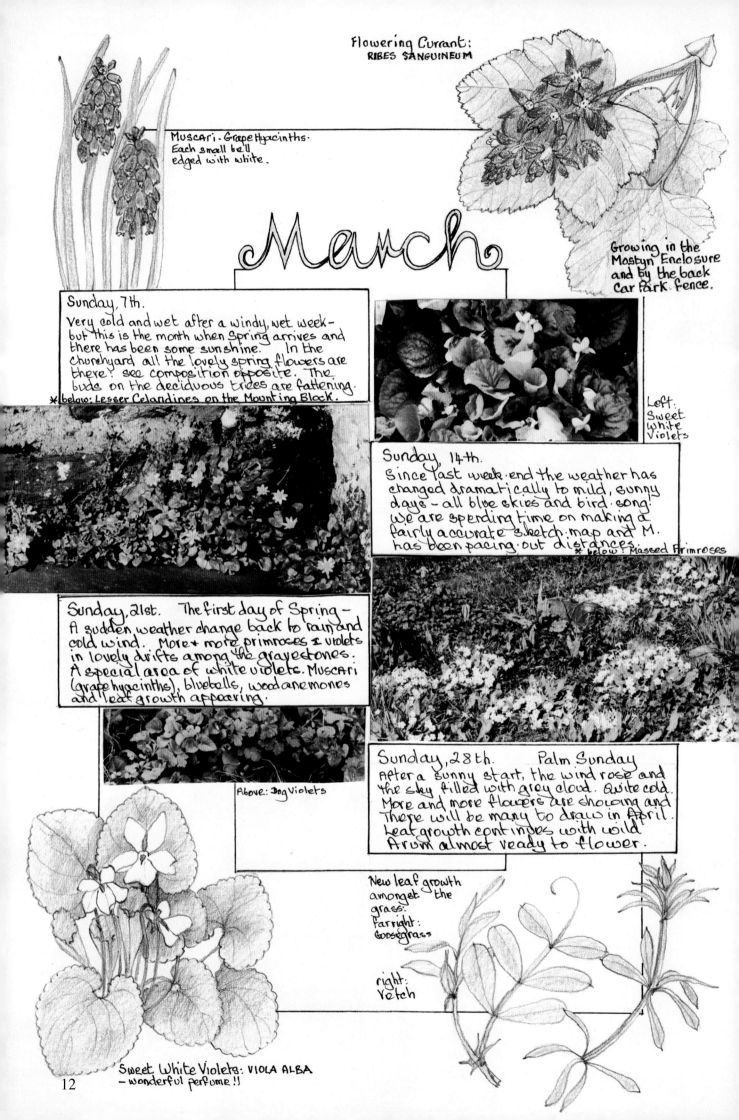

Flowering Currant:
RIBES SANGUINEUM

Muscari - Grape Hyacinths.
Each small bell
edged with white.

March

Growing in the
Mostyn Enclosure
and by the back
Car Park fence.

Sunday, 7th.
Very cold and wet after a windy, wet week -
but this is the month when Spring arrives and
there has been some sunshine.   In the
churchyard all the lovely spring flowers are
there: see composition opposite.   The
buds on the deciduous trees are fattening.
*below: Lesser Celandines on the Mounting Block.

Left:
Sweet
White
Violets

Sunday, 14th.
Since last week.end the weather has
changed dramatically to mild, sunny
days - all blue skies and bird.song!
We are spending time on making a
fairly accurate sketch.map and M.
has been pacing.out distances.
* below: Massed Primroses

Sunday, 21st.   The first day of Spring -
A sudden weather change back to rain and
cold wind.   More + more primroses + violets
in lovely drifts among the gravestones.
A special area of white violets. Muscari
(grape hyacinths), bluebells, wood anemones
and leaf growth appearing.

Above: Dog Violets

Sunday, 28th.   Palm Sunday
After a sunny start, the wind rose and
the sky filled with grey cloud. Quite cold.
More and more flowers are showing and
There will be many to draw in April.
Leaf growth continues with wild
Arum almost ready to flower.

New leaf growth
amongst the
grass.
Far right:
Goosegrass

right:
Vetch

Sweet White Violets: VIOLA ALBA
— wonderful perfume !!

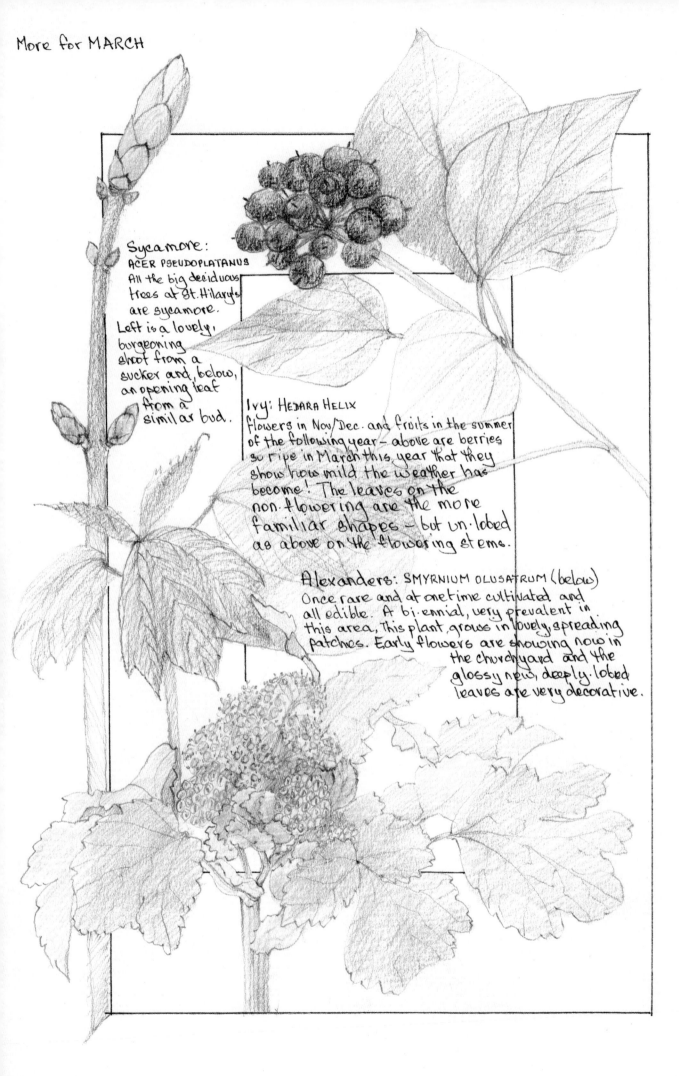

Sycamore:
ACER PSEUDOPLATANUS
All the big deciduous
trees at St. Hilary's
are sycamore.
Left is a lovely,
burgeoning
shoot from a
sucker and, below,
an opening leaf
from a
similar bud.

Ivy: HEDARA HELIX
Flowers in Nov/Dec. and fruits in the summer
of the following year — above are berries
so ripe in March this year that they
show how mild the weather has
become! The leaves on the
non-flowering are the more
familiar shapes — but un-lobed
as above on the flowering stems.

Alexanders: SMYRNIUM OLUSATRUM (below)
Once rare and at one time cultivated and
all edible. A bi-ennial, very prevalent in
this area, this plant grows in lovely spreading
patches. Early flowers are showing now in
the churchyard and the
glossy new, deeply-lobed
leaves are very decorative.

13

Four varieties of Daffodil - the smallest
may be the wild NARCISSUS PSEUDONARCISSUS;
Primroses: PRIMULA VULGARIS;
Lesser Celandine: RANUNCULUS FICARIA;
Common Dog Violet: VIOLA RIVINIANA;
Cultivated scilla - Lily family -
CHIONODOXA.   7 March 1999
                     at St. Hilary's.

Betty Mills

Flowers En Masse

From January until April
various parts of the churchyard
are carpeted by the expected
Spring flowers.
Snowdrop (left) are the first and
are gloriously prolific particularly
in the lower parts, under the trees.
Daffodils (below right) and Primroses,
(bottom left) follow and are in all
areas.
There are some surprises:
Purple Dog Violets (bottom right) &
Sweet White Violets (see page 8)
are widely distributed in the grass
and Common Speedwell (centre left)
grows thickly in the mown area.

more Flowers En Masse:

Above. (Rt.)
Drifts of Forget-me-Nots appear in various areas during April and May.

Above (left):
Alexanders grow thickly in two areas: by the back wall towards the Mostyn enclosure; and against the front, or West wall, beside the mown area.

Right:
Ramsoms grow in one place only: by the south Wall in the lower area. Here they form a thick mass in May - very onion. scented.

Left:
The glory of April and May are, of course, the Bluebells: white & pink as well as blue.
Sited everywhere, they grow very thickly with magnificent blooms.

April

Maundy Thursday, 1st.

Another mild, lovely Spring day.
The primroses are now at their
best in big patches all over the
churchyard - both in the upper, mown
area round the church and in the
more natural, lower area. Dog
and sweet white violets are
also in full flower and much of
the upper area is blue with
Common Field Speedwell.
Have now walked all the paths
and investigated every "nook
and cranny".
Leaf growth amongst the grass,
both cut and untrimmed, and
round the graves promises a
wide variety of flowers to
come.
So far have identified 47 wild
species as well as many cultivated plants plus evergreen
and deciduous trees.

left: Smooth Sowthistle: SONCHUS OLERACEUS
Wallflower: CHEIRANTHUS (cultivated)
and Dandelion: TARAXACUM VULGARE.

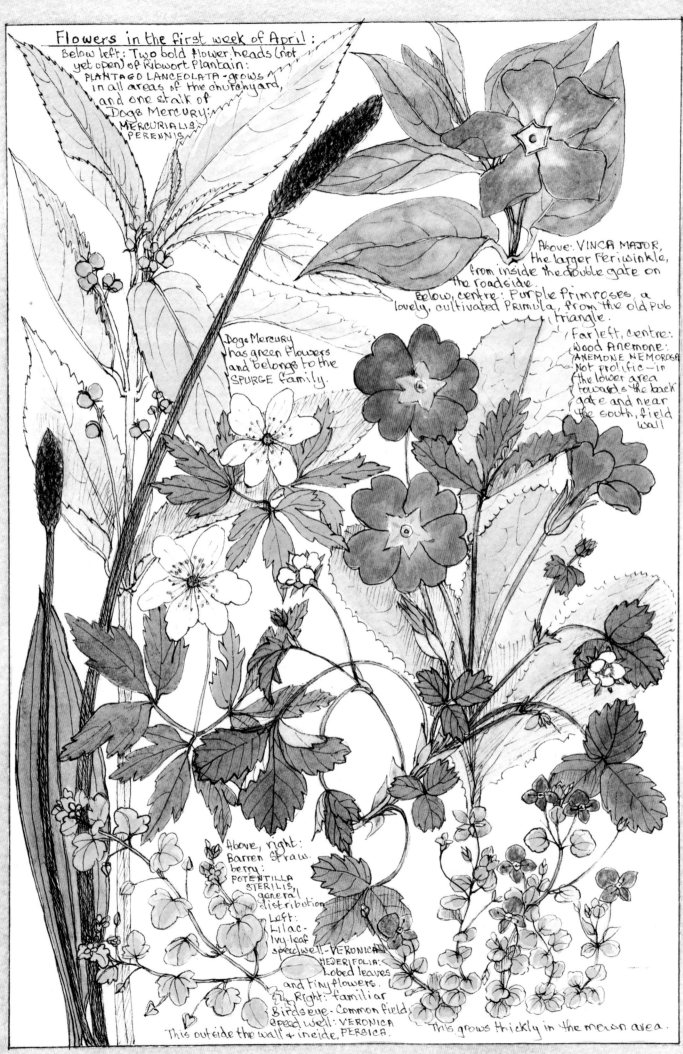

Flowers in the first week of April:
Below left: Two bold flower heads (not yet open) of Ribwort Plantain: PLANTAGO LANCEOLATA - grows in all areas of the churchyard, and one stalk of Dogs Mercury: MERCURIALIS PERENNIS.

Above: VINCA MAJOR, the larger Periwinkle, from inside the double gate on the roadside.
Below, centre: Purple Primroses, a lovely, cultivated Primula, from the old Pub triangle.

Dogs Mercury has green flowers and belongs to the SPURGE family.

Far left, centre: Wood Anemone: ANEMONE NEMOROSA Not prolific - in the lower area towards the back gate and near the south, field wall

Above, right: Barren Straw. berry: POTENTILLA STERILIS, general distribution.
Left: Lilac- Ivy leaf speedwell - VERONICA HEDERIFOLIA: Lobed leaves and tiny flowers.
Right: familiar Birdseye - Common field; speed well: VERONICA PERSICA. This outside the wall + inside.

This grows thickly in the meadow area.

18

April

Sunday, 11th. Easter week has been quite mild with some lovely sunny, spring days but also rain and wind. Today began beautifully but became overcast and rough. Snow is expected in the Scottish Highlands!

The carefully mown grass in the upper part of the churchyard round the church is handled to preserve flowering periods of primroses etc. Common Field Speedwell and ordinary small daisies (BELLIS PERENNIS) thrive on this treatment and become semi-cultivated

See right ——→

The pale yellow anthers - on fine, silvery stalks - start to open up from the bottom of RIBWORT PLANTAIN flowers. As they die off but new ones appear they form the distinctive collar & give off clouds of pollen.

Forget-me-Not: MYOSOTIS sweetly planted on many graves.

The twice-yearly rougher-cutting in the lower areas has a similar, cultivating effect - especially on the Wild Arum which is one of the special treats at St. Hilary's.

Wild Arum:
ARUM MACULATUM or Lords + Ladies.
Cuckoo Pint A. ITALICUM has a yellow spadix.

Sunday, 18th. The snow DID come - lying on the fields right down to the water's edge at Glan Conwy. The mountains were thickly covered. Cold weather persisted all the week with sunshine, more snow showers and heavy rain this morning. But everything continues to grow: the grass has been mown on the upper level and the bluebells are in full flower plus the ransoms.

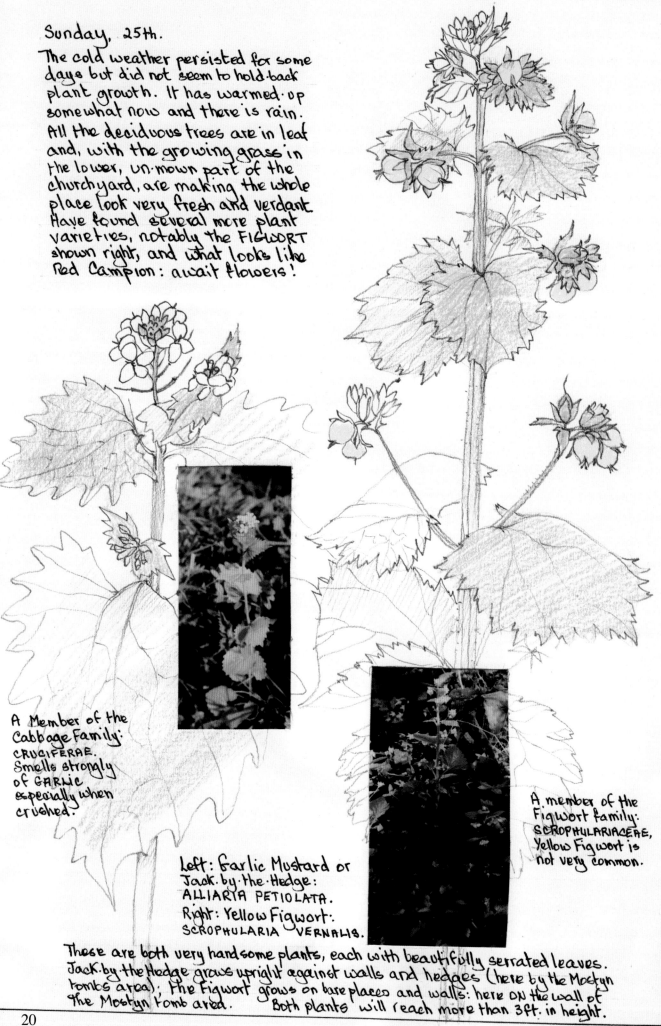

Sunday, 25th.

The cold weather persisted for some days but did not seem to hold back plant growth. It has warmed up somewhat now and there is rain. All the deciduous trees are in leaf and, with the growing grass in the lower, un·mown part of the churchyard, are making the whole place look very fresh and verdant. Have found several more plant varieties, notably the FIGWORT shown right, and what looks like Red Campion: await flowers!

A Member of the Cabbage Family: CRUCIFERAE. Smells strongly of GARLIC especially when crushed.

A member of the Figwort family: SCROPHULARIACEAE, Yellow Figwort is not very common.

Left: Garlic Mustard or Jack·by·the·Hedge: ALLIARIA PETIOLATA.
Right: Yellow Figwort: SCROPHULARIA VERNALIS.

These are both very handsome plants, each with beautifully serrated leaves. Jack·by·the·Hedge grows upright against walls and hedges (here by the Mostyn tombs area). The Figwort grows on bare places and walls: here on the wall of the Mostyn tomb area. Both plants will reach more than 3ft. in height.

Bluebell: ENDYMION NON·SCRIPTUS. These form a wonderful carpet in the unmown area of the churchyard. Varying in colour from deep blue through shades of pink to pure white, they are semi-cultivated.

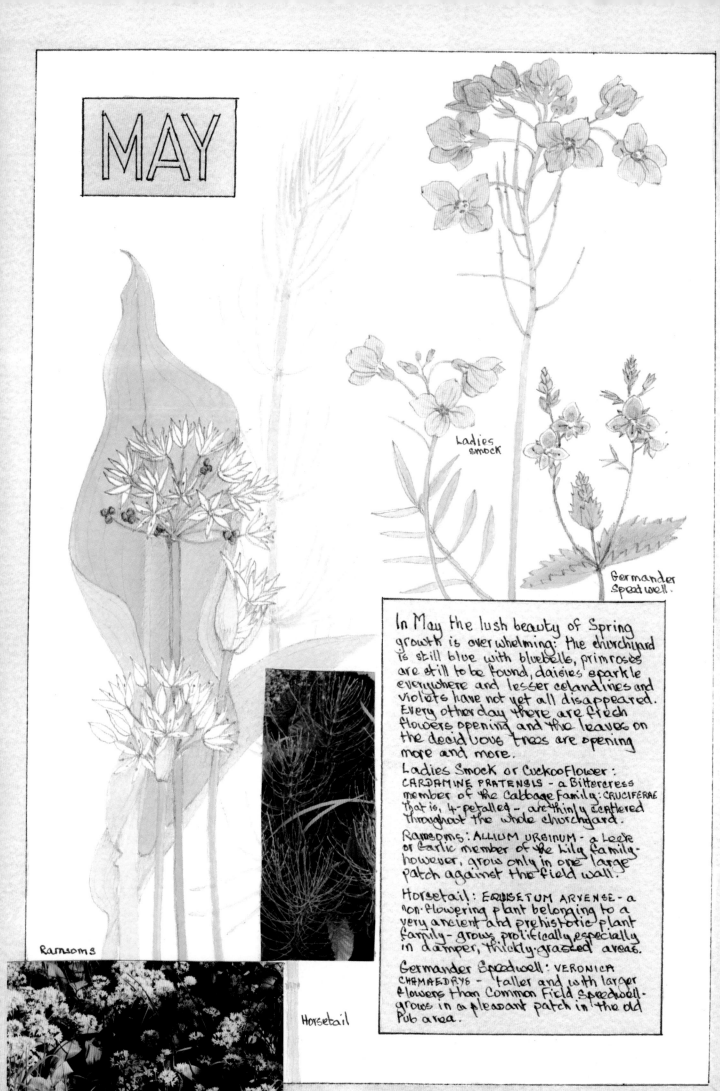

MAY

Ladies
smock

Germander
speedwell.

Ramsoms

Horsetail

In May the lush beauty of Spring
growth is overwhelming: the churchyard
is still blue with bluebells, primroses
are still to be found, daisies sparkle
everywhere and lesser celandines and
violets have not yet all disappeared.
Every other day there are fresh
flowers opening and the leaves on
the deciduous trees are opening
more and more.

Ladies Smock or Cuckoo Flower:
CARDAMINE PRATENSIS - a Bittercress
member of the Cabbage family: CRUCIFERAE
that is, 4-petalled - are thinly scattered
throughout the whole churchyard.

Ramsoms: ALLIUM URSINUM - a Leek
or Garlic member of the Lily family.
however, grow only in one large
patch against the field wall.

Horsetail: EQUISETUM ARVENSE - a
non-flowering plant belonging to a
very ancient and prehistoric plant
family - grows prolifically especially
in damper, thickly grassed areas.

Germander Speedwell: VERONICA
CHAMAEDRYS - taller and with larger
flowers than Common Field Speedwell.
grows in a pleasant patch in the old
Pub area.

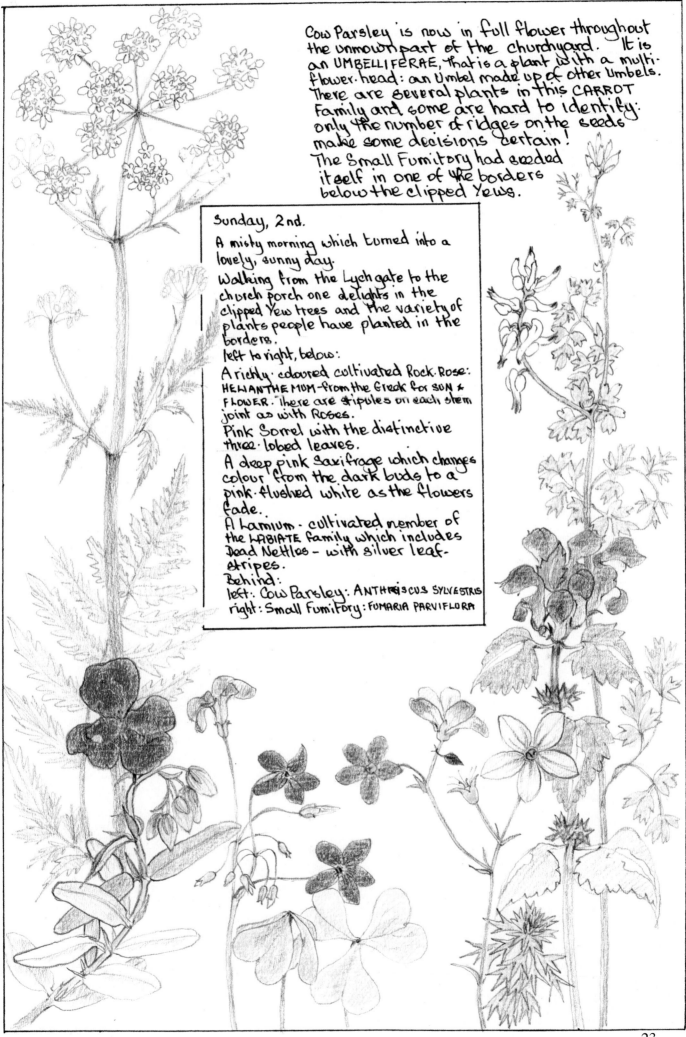

Cow Parsley is now in full flower throughout
the unmown part of the churchyard. It is
an UMBELLIFERAE, that is a plant with a multi-
flower-head: an Umbel made up of other Umbels.
There are several plants in this CARROT
family and some are hard to identify:
only the number of ridges on the seeds
make some decisions certain!
The Small Fumitory had seeded
itself in one of the borders
below the clipped Yews.

Sunday, 2nd.

A misty morning which turned into a
lovely, sunny day.

Walking from the Lych gate to the
church porch one delights in the
clipped Yew trees and the variety of
plants people have planted in the
borders.

left to right, below:

A richly-coloured cultivated Rock-Rose:
HELIANTHEMUM - from the Greek for SUN &
FLOWER. There are stipules on each stem
joint as with Roses.

Pink Sorrel with the distinctive
three-lobed leaves.

A deep pink Saxifrage which changes
colour from the dark buds to a
pink-flushed white as the flowers
fade.

A Lamium - cultivated member of
the LABIATE family which includes
Dead Nettles - with silver leaf-
stripes.

Behind:

left: Cow Parsley: ANTHRISCUS SYLVESTRIS
right: Small Fumitory: FUMARIA PARVIFLORA

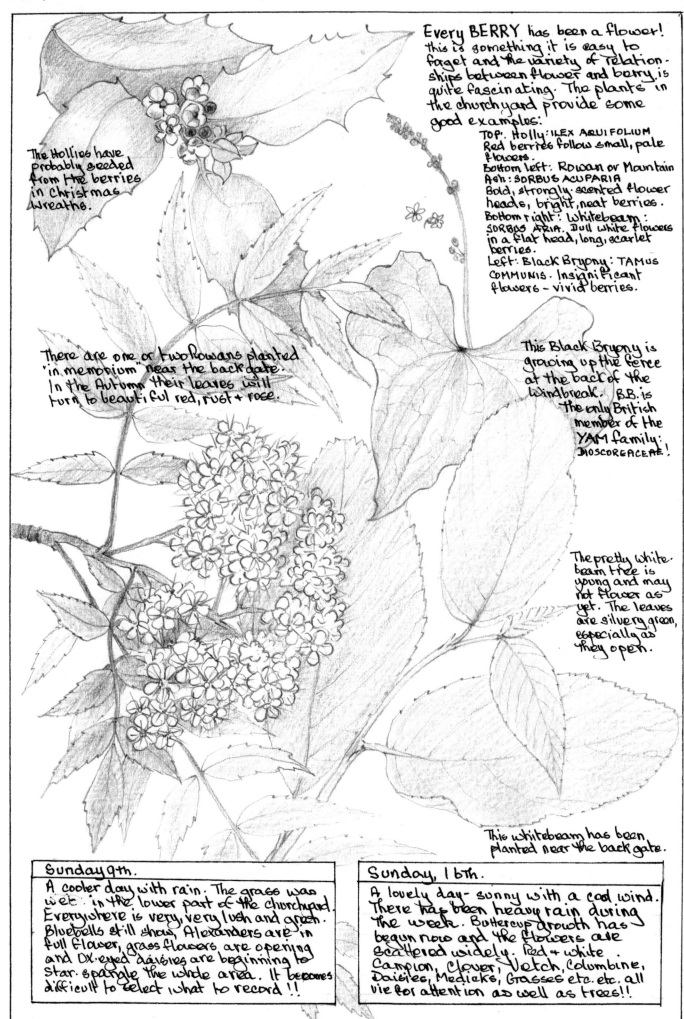

The Hollies have probably seeded from the berries in Christmas wreaths.

Every BERRY has been a flower! this is something it is easy to forget and the variety of relationships between flower and berry is quite fascinating. The plants in the churchyard provide some good examples:

TOP: Holly: ILEX AQUIFOLIUM Red berries follow small, pale flowers.

Bottom left: Rowan or Mountain Ash: SORBUS ACUPARIA Bold, strongly-scented flower heads, bright, neat berries.

Bottom right: Whitebeam: SORBUS ARIA. Dull white flowers in a flat head, long, scarlet berries.

Left: Black Bryony: TAMUS COMMUNIS. Insignificant flowers - vivid berries.

There are one or two Rowans planted "in memorium" near the back gate. In the Autumn their leaves will turn to beautiful red, rust + rose.

This Black Bryony is growing up the fence at the back of the windbreak. B.B. is the only British member of the YAM family: DIOSCOREACEAE!

The pretty whitebeam tree is young and may not flower as yet. The leaves are silvery green, especially as they open.

This whitebeam has been planted near the back gate.

Sunday 9th.
A cooler day with rain. The grass was wet in the lower part of the churchyard. Everywhere is very, very lush and green. Bluebells still show, Alexanders are in full flower, grass flowers are opening and Ox-eyed daisies are beginning to star-spangle the whole area. It becomes difficult to select what to record !!

Sunday, 16th.
A lovely day- sunny with a cool wind. There has been heavy rain during the week. Buttercup growth has begun now and the flowers are scattered widely. Red + white Campion, Clover, Vetch, Columbine, Daisies, Medicks, Grasses etc. etc. all vie for attention as well as trees!!

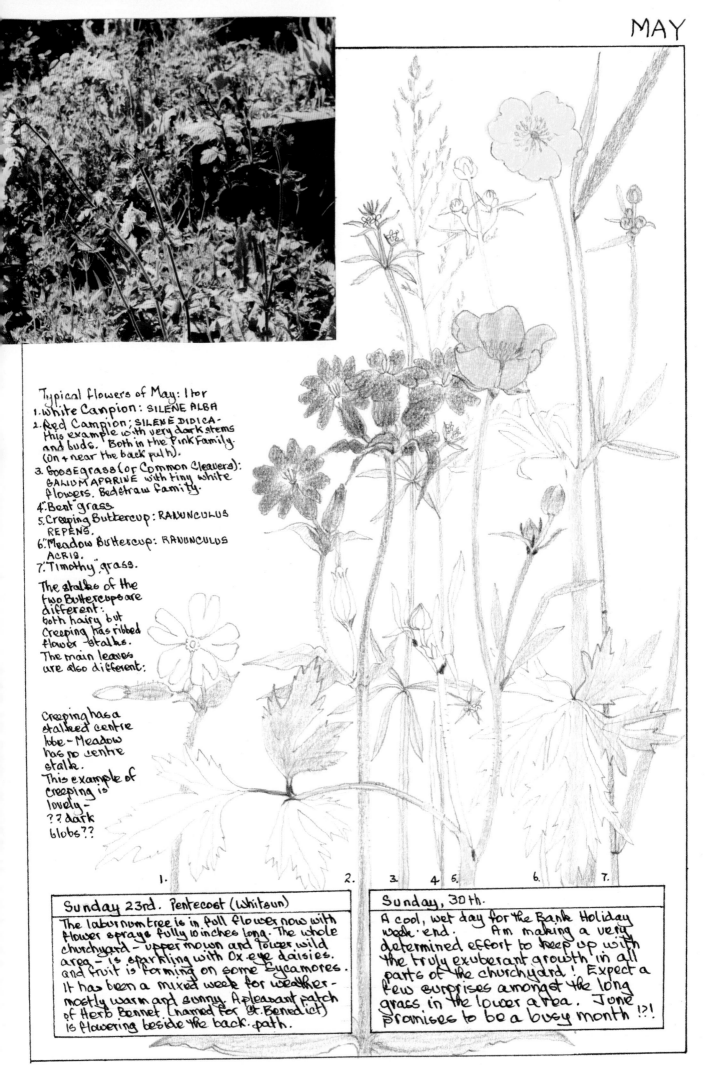

Typical flowers of May: I for

1. White Campion: SILENE ALBA
2. Red Campion: SILENE DIOICA - this example with very dark stems and buds. Both in the Pink Family. (On + near the back path).
3. Goosegrass (or Common Cleavers): GALIUM APARINE with tiny white flowers. Bedstraw family.
4. "Bent" grass
5. Creeping Buttercup: RANUNCULUS REPENS.
6. Meadow Buttercup: RANUNCULUS ACRIS.
7. "Timothy" grass.

The stalks of the two Buttercups are different: both hairy but Creeping has ribbed flower stalks. The main leaves are also different:

Creeping has a stalked centre lobe - Meadow has no centre stalk. This example of creeping is lovely - ?? dark blobs??

1.   2.   3.   4 5.   6.   7.

Sunday 23rd. Pentecost (Whitsun)

The laburnum tree is in full flower now with flower sprays fully 10 inches long. The whole churchyard - upper mown and lower wild area - is sparkling with Ox-eye daisies and fruit is forming on some Sycamores. It has been a mixed week for weather - mostly warm and sunny. A pleasant patch of Herb Bennet (named for St. Benedict) is flowering beside the back path.

Sunday, 30th.

A cool, wet day for the Bank Holiday week-end. Am making a very determined effort to keep up with the truly exuberant growth in all parts of the churchyard! Expect a few surprises amongst the long grass in the lower area. June promises to be a busy month!?!

25

More bounteous growth this month.

Right: A small sprig of English Yew, with fresh leaf growth and an incipient berry.

The deciduous trees are now, almost all, in full leaf.
Left: A sycamore flower with, drawn near the tip of the hanging cluster, a
✳ single flower with the distinctive winged seed already showing.
The photograph, right, shows the big sycamore near the church porch still red·gold as its opening leaves are later than the one behind.

Flowers - left to right below:
Columbine: AQUILEGIA VULGARIS (may be cultivated).
Daisy: BELLIS PERENNIS, now at their best in the grass.
Red Clover: TRIFOLIUM PRATENSE.
Black Medick: MEDICAGO LUPULINA

✳

Common Vetch: VICIA SATIVA - this grows in every area of the churchyard and, together with the Clover & the Medick is in the PEA family - a LEGUMINOSAE

This is a Yellow Crucifer, ie. 4·petalled, in the Cabbage Family.
A base leaf is needed to get correct naming:
Annual Wall Rocket: DIPLOTAXIS MURALIS.

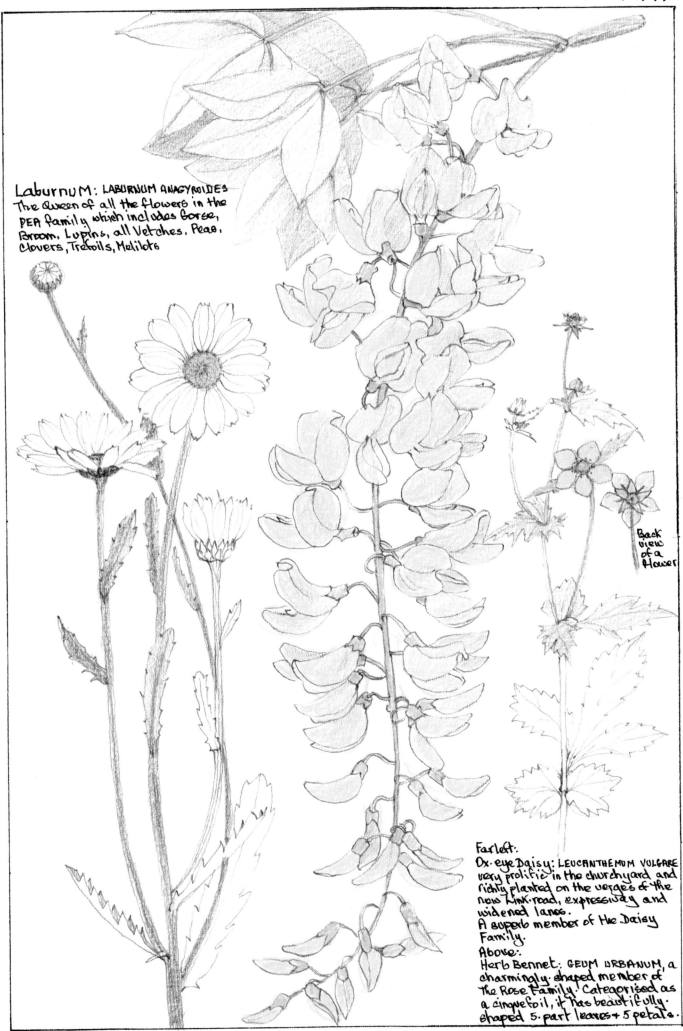

Laburnum: LABURNUM ANAGYROIDES
The Queen of all the flowers in the
PEA family which includes Gorse,
Broom, Lupins, all Vetches, Peas,
Clovers, Trefoils, Melilots

Back
view
of a
flower

Far left:
Ox eye Daisy: LEUCANTHEMUM VULGARE
very prolific in the churchyard and
richly planted on the verges of the
new Link·road, expressway and
widened lanes.
A superb member of the Daisy
Family.
Above:
Herb Bennet: GEUM URBANUM, a
charmingly·shaped member of
the Rose Family. Categorised as
a cinquefoil, it has beautifully·
shaped 5·part leaves + 5 petals.

Bold leaves: spears which clasp the stems and pointed pairs.

June

Greyer leaves.

The month comes in with an almost embarrassing richness of flower growth!
Two groups are illustrated:
First-
Three CRANESBILLS - so-called because of the shape of their seeds- members of the GERANIUM FAMILY.
Below left: a cultivated Cranesbill from the Lychgate border.
Behind it: Hedgerow Cranes-bill: GERANIUM PYRENAICUM
below, right: Herb Robert: G. ROBERTIANUM.
The Three yellow flowers are from the PEA FAMILY.
Top left: Meadow Vetchling: LATHYRUS PRATENSIS,
Top right: Greater Bird's Foot Trefoil: LOTUS ULIGINOSUS &
below Birdsfoot Trefoil.
LOTUS CORNICULATUS

Tiny Mauve flowers.

Softer leaves

IN BLACK PEN ROUND THE BORDER:
Hairy Tare: VICIA HIRSUTA,
a pale mauve VETCH.

Seed pods.

Elder:
SAMBUCUS
NIGRA

Sunday, 6th.
D. day for those of us who
remember 1944!
After a mixed week for weather-
pouring wet day on Wednesday-
it's now cooler and still very
showery. Growth in the
churchyard continues apace
with tree flowers now almost
all out. See Elderberry, above.
Two members of the Nettle
family (URTICACEAE) shown here:
        Far left:
        Pellitory of the Wall:
        PARIETARIA JUDAICA,
        not stinging but hairy
        and grows in, on or near
        walls. Very common
        locally.
        Right: Stinging Nettle:
URTICA DIOICA - male
+ female flowers, on different
plants. Easily reaches 3 feet
tall with 3 inch leaves if left
to flourish.
Left:
Goatsbeard or Jack go to bed
at noon (because they do!).
TRAGOPOGON PRATENSIS - a plant
of great charm: vigorous and
upright with leaves like fine
spears clothing the stem. The
flowers are solitary and the
seedheads a very large "clock."
Below, centre:
Ivy leaved Toadflax: CYMBALARIA
MURALIS - a fig wort family member growing on walls.
Below left: Cultivated Corn
flower, Calendula (Marigold)
and Aubretia.

29

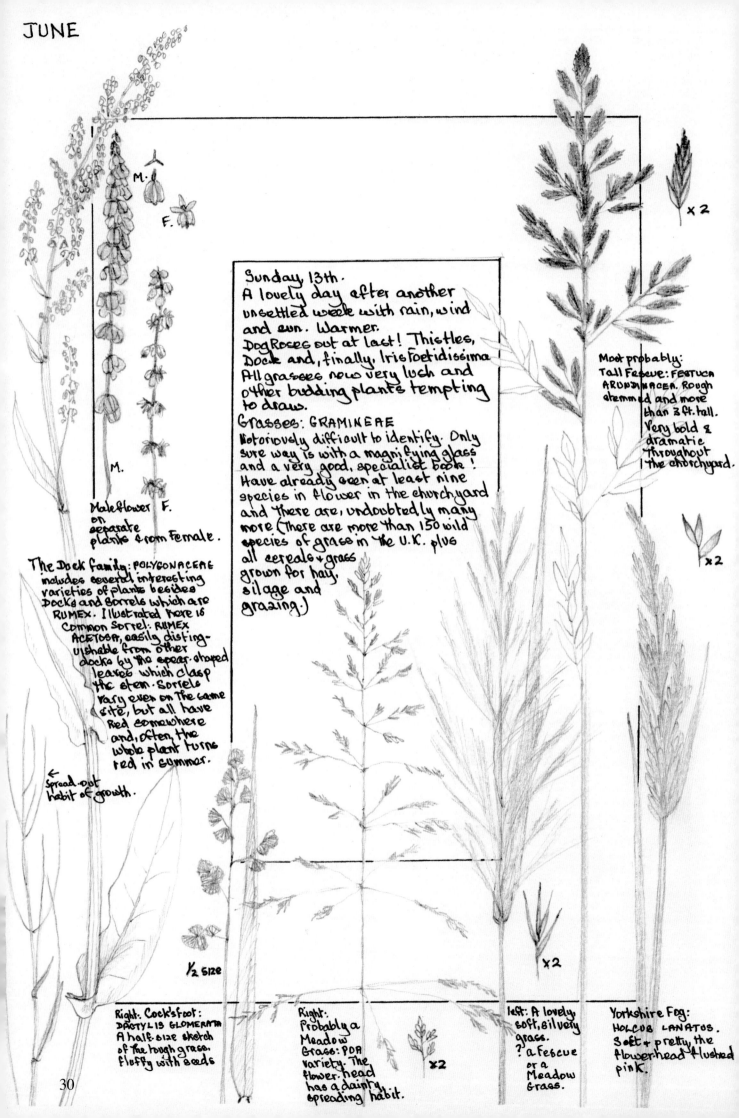

Sunday, 13th.
A lovely day after another unsettled week with rain, wind and sun. Warmer.
Dog Roses out at last! Thistles, Dock and, finally, Iris Foetidissima
All grasses now very lush and other budding plants tempting to draw.

Grasses: GRAMINEAE
Notoriously difficult to identify. Only sure way is with a magnifying glass and a very good, specialist book! Have already seen at least nine species in flower in the churchyard and there are, undoubtedly many more (There are more than 150 wild species of grass in the U.K. plus all cereals + grass grown for hay, silage and grazing.)

M. ♂
F. ♀

M.

Male flower F. on separate plants from Female.

The Dock family: POLYGONACEAE includes several interesting varieties of plants besides Docks and Sorrels which are RUMEX. Illustrated here is Common Sorrel: RUMEX ACETOSA, easily disting-uishable from other docks by the spear-shaped leaves which clasp the stem. Sorrels vary even on the same site, but all have Red somewhere and, often the whole plant turns red in summer.

← Spread-out habit of growth.

½ size

Most probably: Tall Fescue: FESTUCA ARUNDINACEA. Rough stemmed and more than 3 ft. tall. Very bold & dramatic throughout the churchyard.

×2

×2

×2

Right: Cock'sfoot: DACTYLIS GLOMERATA A half-size sketch of the tough grass. fluffy with seeds

Right: Probably a Meadow Grass: POA variety. The flower head has a dainty spreading habit.

×2

left: A lovely soft, silvery grass. ? a Fescue or a Meadow Grass.

Yorkshire Fog: HOLCUS LANATUS. Soft + pretty, the flowerhead flushed pink.

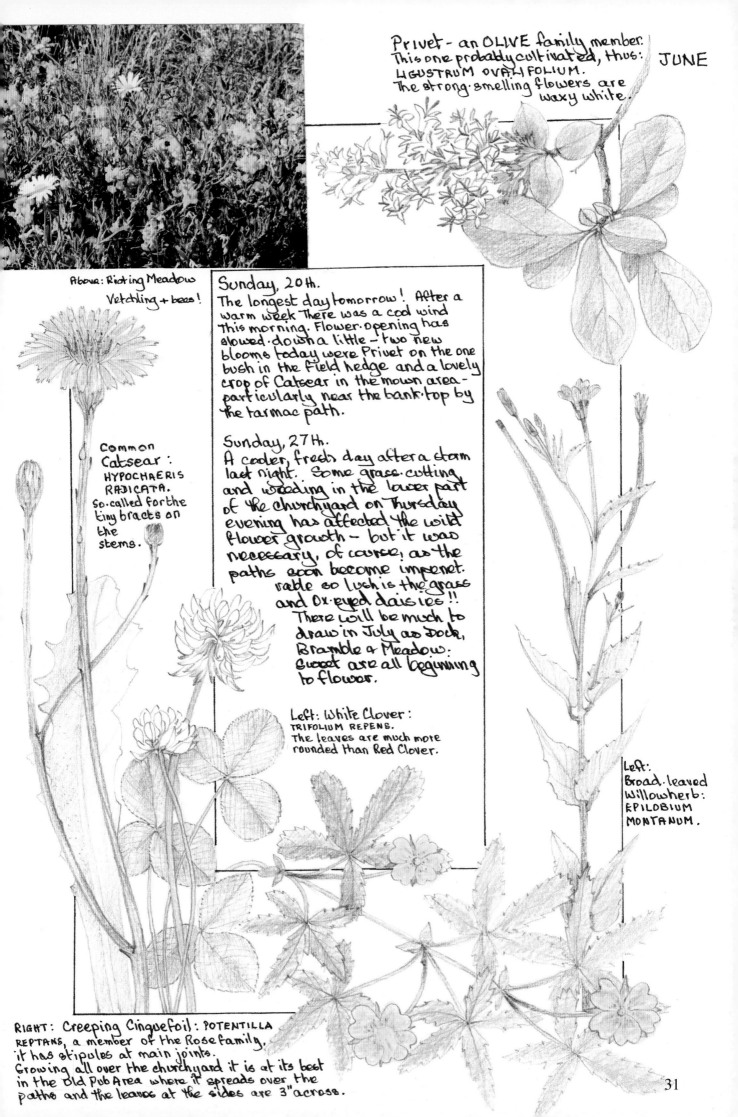

Privet - an OLIVE family member.
This one probably cultivated, thus:
LIGUSTRUM OVALIFOLIUM.
The strong-smelling flowers are
waxy white.

Above: Rioting Meadow
Vetchling + bees!

Common
Catsear:
HYPOCHAERIS
RADICATA.
So-called for the
tiny bracts on
the
stems.

Sunday, 20th.
The longest day tomorrow! After a
warm week there was a cool wind
this morning. Flower-opening has
slowed-down a little - two new
blooms today were Privet on the one
bush in the field-hedge and a lovely
crop of Catsear in the mown area -
particularly near the bank-top by
the tarmac path.

Sunday, 27th.
A cooler, fresh day after a storm
last night. Some grass-cutting
and weeding in the lower part
of the churchyard on Thursday
evening has affected the wild
flower growth - but it was
necessary, of course, as the
paths soon become impenet-
rable so lush is the grass
and Ox-eyed daisies!!
There will be much to
draw in July as Dock,
Bramble & Meadow-
Sweet are all beginning
to flower.

Left: White Clover:
TRIFOLIUM REPENS.
The leaves are much more
rounded than Red Clover.

Left:
Broad-leaved
Willowherb:
EPILOBIUM
MONTANUM.

RIGHT: Creeping Cinquefoil: POTENTILLA
REPTANS, a member of the Rose family,
it has stipules at main joints.
Growing all over the churchyard it is at its best
in the old Pub Area where it spreads over the
paths and the leaves at the sides are 3" across.

31

Centre back: Hedge Woundwort: STACHYS SYLVATICA;
Right back: Creeping Thistle: CIRSIUM ARVENSE.
Centre: Iris FOETIDISSIMA, flowering now all over
the Churchyard to form the distinctive berries.
Left foreground: Field Rose: ROSA ARVENSIS and,
right, Dog Rose: ROSA CANINA both from the back
Car Park fence.

The prolific and uninhibited growth of the wild plants in the lower part of the churchyard does make it no easy matter to maintain access to many of the graves— BUT, the free growth looks beautiful!

above:
Ox-eye Daisies growing unrestricted.

Right:
Young sycamore plants and young Horsetail glow against a granite tomb.

below:
Red + white campion and, Bottom right, more sycamore + ivy.

33

Rich, high summer growth and strong lighting combine with good photography to produce three dramatic shots of Hogweed and a well-composed view of an Elderberry bush.

July

Meadowsweet:
FILIPENDULA ULMARIA, a member of the Rose family.

Sunday, 4th.–warm + sunny
This is a month of high summer when the leaves of the deciduous trees are settling to a darker green after the spring freshness. Some are already fruiting eg. the Sycamores. It is also a time of big, bold flower-heads in the fields and hedgerows.
In the churchyard Meadowsweet, Common Hogweed and Dock are good examples with more to come if they can escape the necessary strimming which has now begun in the lower part of the churchyard.

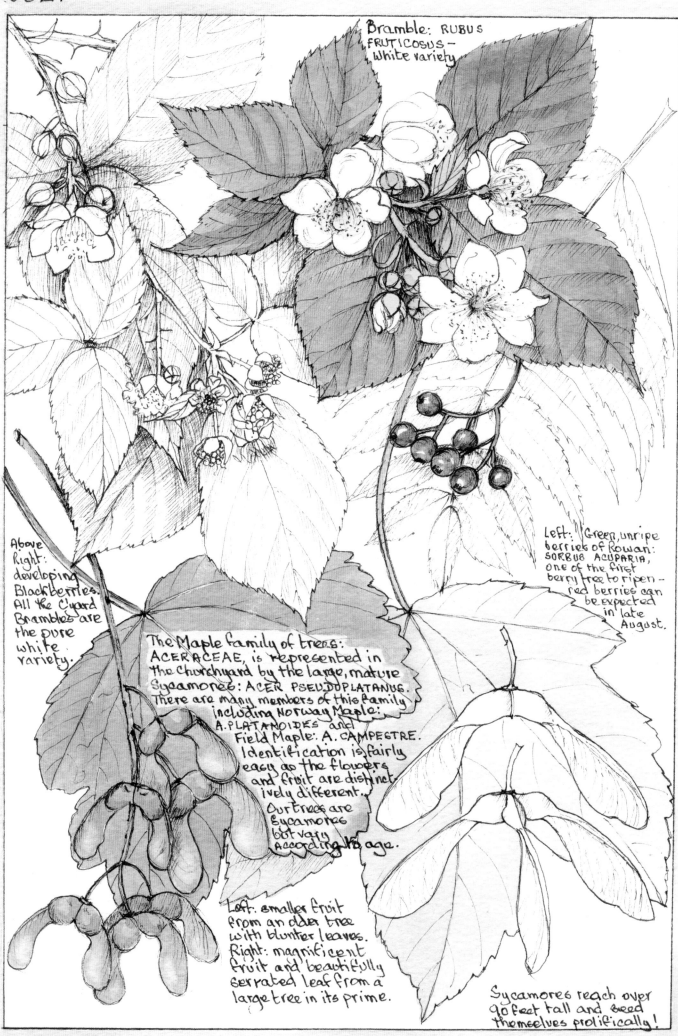

Bramble: RUBUS FRUTICOSUS – white variety

Left: Green, unripe berries of Rowan: SORBUS ACUPARIA, one of the first berry tree to ripen – red berries can be expected in late August.

Above Right: developing Blackberries. All the Cyard Brambles are the pure white variety.

The Maple family of trees: ACERACEAE, is represented in the Churchyard by the large, mature Sycamores: ACER PSEUDOPLATANUS. There are many members of this family including Norway Maple: A. PLATANOIDES and Field Maple: A. CAMPESTRE. Identification is fairly easy as the flowers and fruit are distinctively different. Our trees are Sycamores but vary according to age.

Left: smaller fruit from an older tree with blunter leaves. Right: magnificent fruit and beautifully serrated leaf from a large tree in its prime.

Sycamores reach over 90 feet tall and seed themselves prolifically!

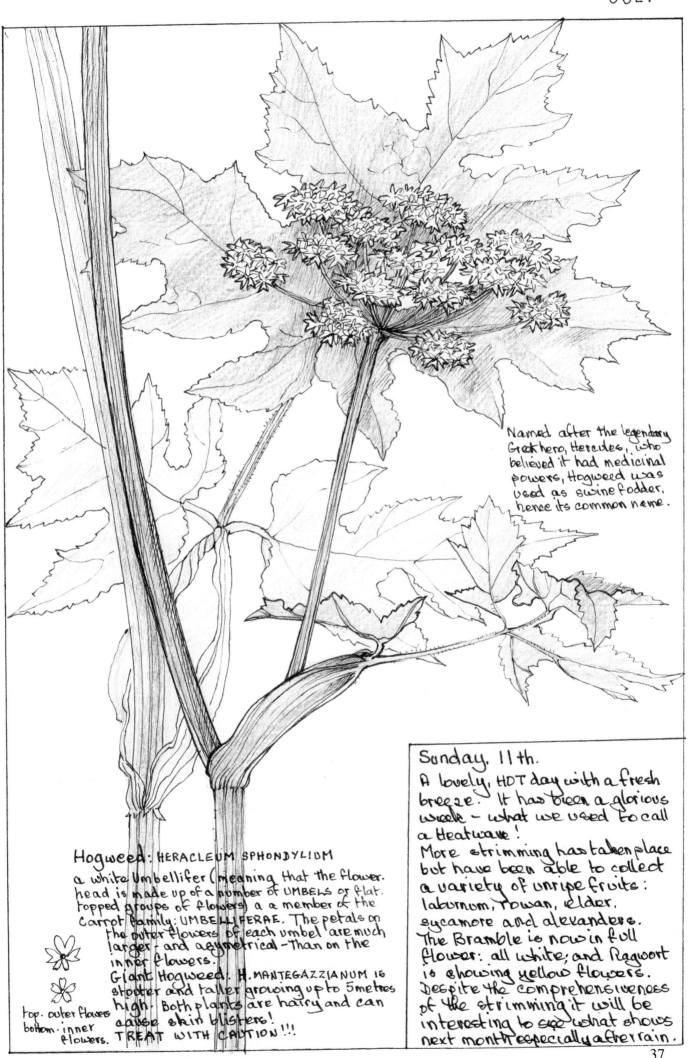

Named after the legendary Greek hero, Hercules, who believed it had medicinal powers, Hogweed was used as swine fodder, hence its common name.

Hogweed: HERACLEUM SPHONDYLIUM
a white Umbellifer (meaning that the flower head is made up of a number of UMBELS or flat-topped groups of flowers) a a member of the carrot family: UMBELLIFERAE. The petals on the outer flowers of each umbel are much larger - and asymetrical - than on the inner flowers.
Giant Hogweed. H. MANTEGAZZIANUM is stouter and taller growing up to 5 metres high. Both plants are hairy and can cause skin blisters! TREAT WITH CAUTION!!!

top. outer flowers
bottom. inner flowers.

Sunday. 11th.
A lovely, HOT day with a fresh breeze. It has been a glorious week - what we used to call a Heatwave!
More strimming has taken place but have been able to collect a variety of unripe fruits: laburnum, rowan, elder, sycamore and alexanders.
The Bramble is now in full flower: all white; and Ragwort is showing yellow flowers. Despite the comprehensiveness of the strimming it will be interesting to see what shows next month especially after rain.

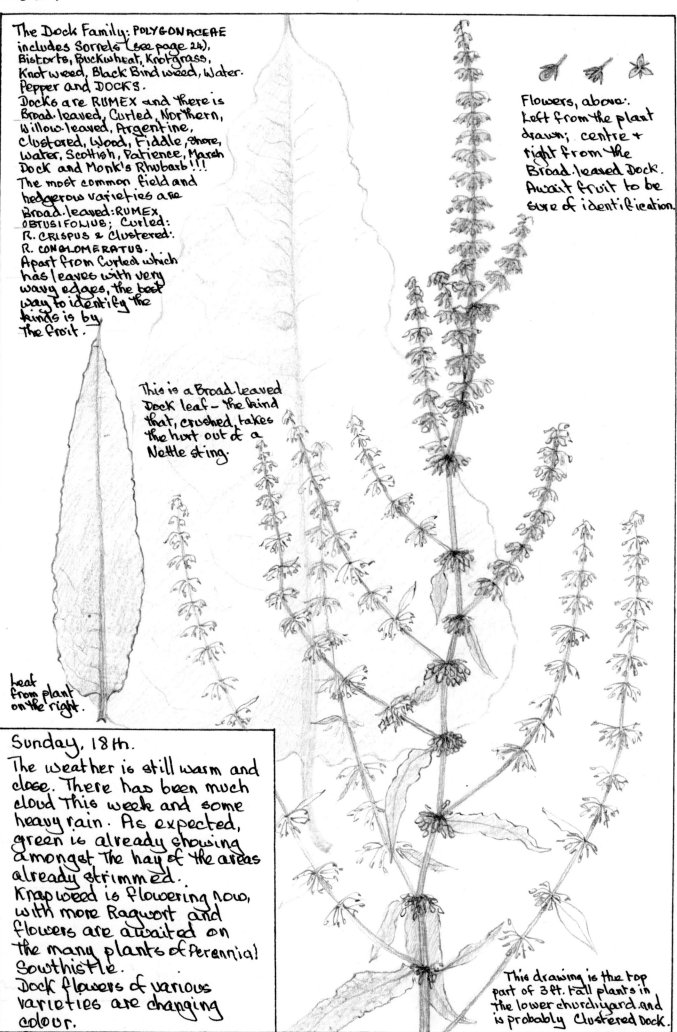

The Dock Family: POLYGONACEAE includes Sorrels (see page 24), Bistorts, Buckwheat, Knotgrass, Knotweed, Black Bindweed, Water Pepper and DOCKS.

Docks are RUMEX and there is Broad-leaved, Curled, Northern, Willow-leaved, Argentine, Clustered, Wood, Fiddle, Shore, Water, Scottish, Patience, Marsh Dock and Monk's Rhubarb!!!

The most common field and hedgerow varieties are Broad-leaved: RUMEX OBTUSIFOLIUS; Curled: R. CRISPUS & Clustered: R. CONGLOMERATUS.

Apart from Curled which has leaves with very wavy edges, the best way to identify the kinds is by the fruit.

This is a Broad-leaved Dock leaf – the kind that, crushed, takes the hurt out of a Nettle sting.

Leaf from plant on the right.

Flowers, above: Left from the plant drawn; centre + right from the Broad-leaved Dock. Await fruit to be sure of identification.

Sunday, 18th.

The weather is still warm and close. There has been much cloud this week and some heavy rain. As expected, green is already showing amongst the hay of the areas already strimmed.

Knapweed is flowering now, with more Ragwort and flowers are awaited on the many plants of Perennial Sowthistle.

Dock flowers of various varieties are changing colour.

This drawing is the top part of 3ft. tall plants in the lower churchyard and is probably Clustered Dock.

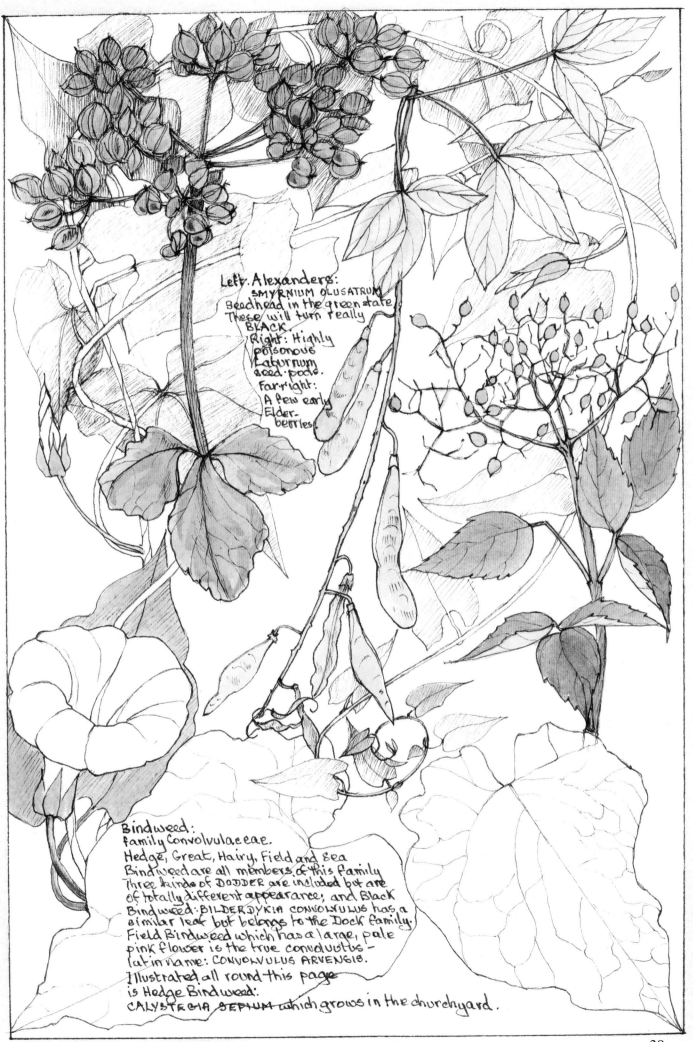

Left. Alexanders:
SMYRNIUM OLUSATRUM
Seedhead in the green state.
These will turn really
BLACK.
Right: Highly
poisonous
Laburnum
seed pods.
Far right:
A few early
Elder-
berries.

Bindweed:
family Convolvulaceae.
Hedge, Great, Hairy, Field and Sea
Bindweed are all members of this family.
Three kinds of DODDER are included but are
of totally different appearance; and Black
Bindweed: BILDERDYKIA CONVOLVULUS has a
similar leaf but belongs to the Dock family.
Field Bindweed which has a large, pale
pink flower is the true convolvulus -
latin name: CONVOLVULUS ARVENSIS.
Illustrated all round this page
is Hedge Bindweed:
CALYSTEGIA SEPIUM which grows in the churchyard.

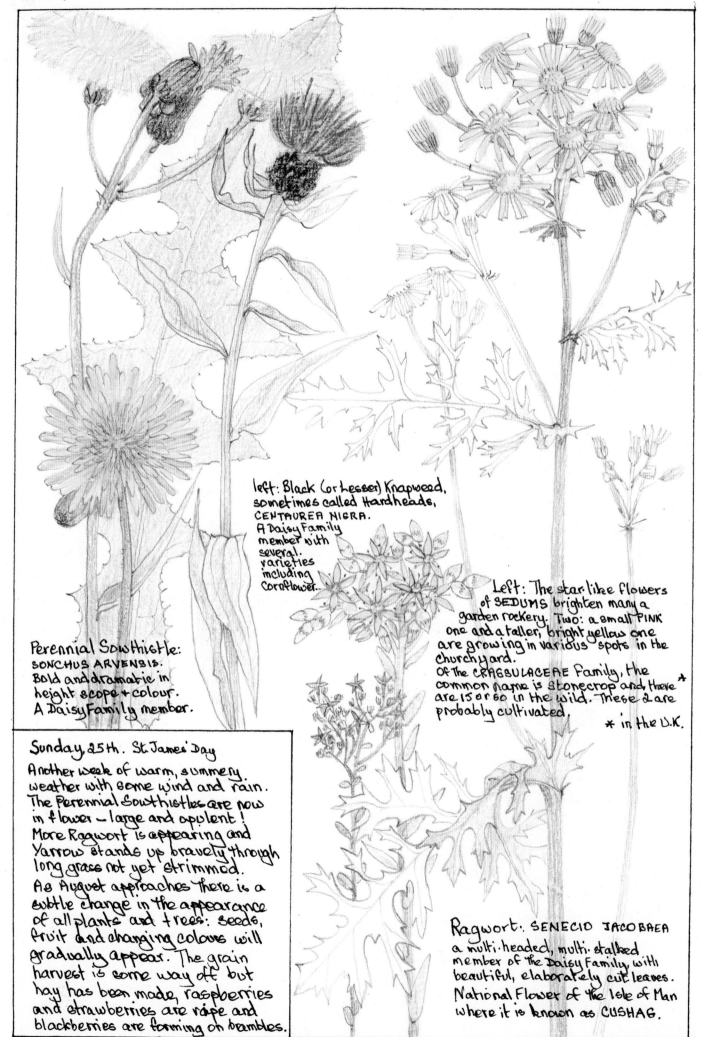

left: Black (or Lesser) Knapweed, sometimes called Hardheads, CENTAUREA NIGRA. A Daisy Family member with several varieties including Cornflower.

Perennial Sowthistle: SONCHUS ARVENSIS. Bold and dramatic in height scope + colour. A Daisy Family member.

Left: The star-like flowers of SEDUMS brighten many a garden rockery. Two: a small PINK one and a taller, bright yellow one are growing in various spots in the churchyard. Of the CRASSULACEAE family, the common name is stonecrop and there * are 15 or so in the wild. These 2 are probably cultivated.

* in the U.K.

Sunday, 25th. St. James' Day

Another week of warm, summery weather with some wind and rain. The Perennial Sowthistles are now in flower – large and opulent! More Ragwort is appearing and Yarrow stands up bravely through long grass not yet strimmed. As August approaches there is a subtle change in the appearance of all plants and trees: seeds, fruit and changing colours will gradually appear. The grain harvest is some way off but hay has been made, raspberries and strawberries are ripe and blackberries are forming on brambles.

Ragwort. SENECIO JACOBAEA a multi-headed, multi-stalked member of the Daisy Family, with beautiful, elaborately cut leaves. National Flower of the Isle of Man where it is known as CUSHAG.

August

Sunday, 1st
A warm, windless, misty day.
Thunder rumbling round after lunch.
Rain is much needed but may be too
heavy if it comes, and just run off
the surface of the dry ground.
Only one area of the lower church-
yard remains to be strimmed and
there the Yarrow and Knapweed
are in full flower.
Lanes around the area are edged
with thickly flowering Ragwort,
Yarrow, Knapweed, Willow herbs,
Fennel, Meadowsweet and Hogweed.
Only some of these grow in the
churchyard.

A pretty Spiraea, probably S. SALICIFOLIA
growing on the wall-top near the roadside gate.

Yarrow:
ACHILLEA MILLEFOLIUM
'Thousand Flowers'

Thistles are members
of the Daisy Family and
fall into two main
groups: CARDUUS and
CIRSIUM although
there are others such
as Carline thistle.

So far have shown two
varieties in the C'yard:
This one: Spear Thistle:
CIRSIUM VULGARE and
Creeping T. on page 26.

41

The path from the Lych-gate to the church porch runs between 17 of the 27 clipped Irish Yews. (The other 10 are alongside the paths to right and left by the porch.) Over the years an herbaceous border has been developed beside the path and there are flowers in it throughout the year.

The Herbaceous Borders in August: 1 for: Berries on Hypericum, White Esthorides, Blue campanulas and Mauve Perennial Asters.

Sunday, 8th.
A day of mixed weather— some rain, some sun.
The Herbaceous borders, pictured above, are a delightful feature in the churchyard. There is colour in them all the year round from the heather and Iris berries in January, wallflowers in April, Helianthemums in May, etc plus Poppies, Cornflowers etc. to early daisies at Xmas.

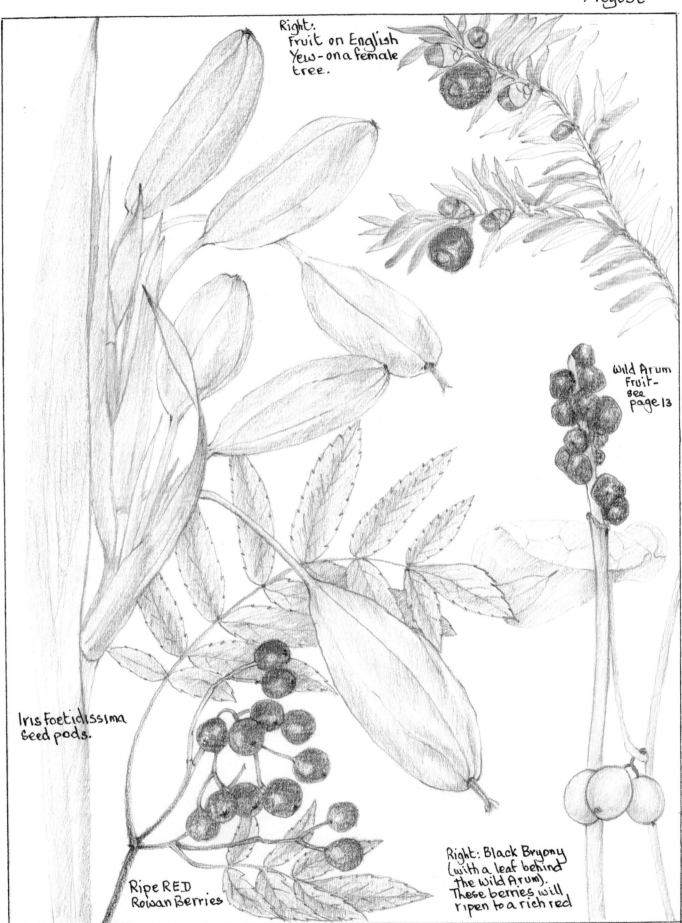

Right.
Fruit on English
Yew - on a female
tree.

Wild Arum
Fruit-
see
page 13

Iris Foetidissima
Seed pods.

Ripe RED
Rowan Berries

Right: Black Bryony
(with a leaf behind
the Wild Arum).
These berries will
ripen to a rich red

Sunday, 15th.
[Away from home so cannot record the weather – heard there was a severe storm on the 14th.] Returning on the 14th, toured the churchyard next day. Many plants are fruiting: Rowan & Yew with red berries; Iris with fat green pods; Black Bryony with green berries - still to ripen. Various kinds of Fungi had appeared; Wild Arum berries are ripe. Not many flowers to be seen except for Rosebay Willowherb and some second flowerings.

43

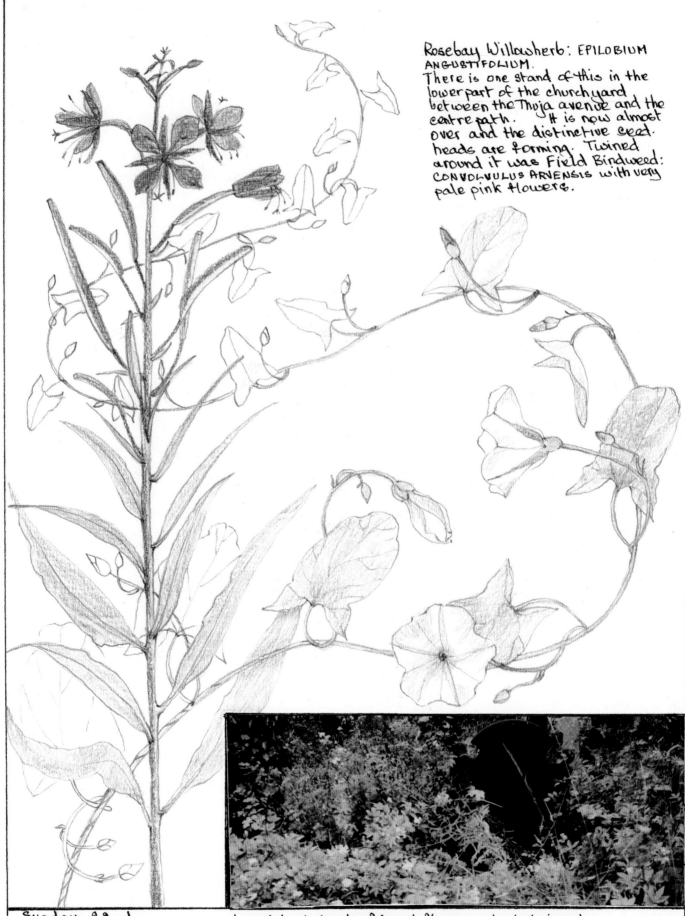

Rosebay Willowherb: EPILOBIUM ANGUSTIFOLIUM.
There is one stand of this in the lower part of the churchyard between the Thuja avenue and the centre path. It is now almost over and the distinctive seed heads are forming. Twined around it was Field Bindweed: CONVOLVULUS ARVENSIS with very pale pink flowers.

above: A lovely tangle of August flowers - not yet strimmed.

Sunday, 22nd.
A lovely, sunny morning with a fresh breeze.
More mushrooms had appeared in the corner of the back car park. The berries on the smaller Rowan tree, which are not the red variety, are fatter and whiter. Many plants in the strimmed area are beginning second flowerings, particularly daisies and red campion.

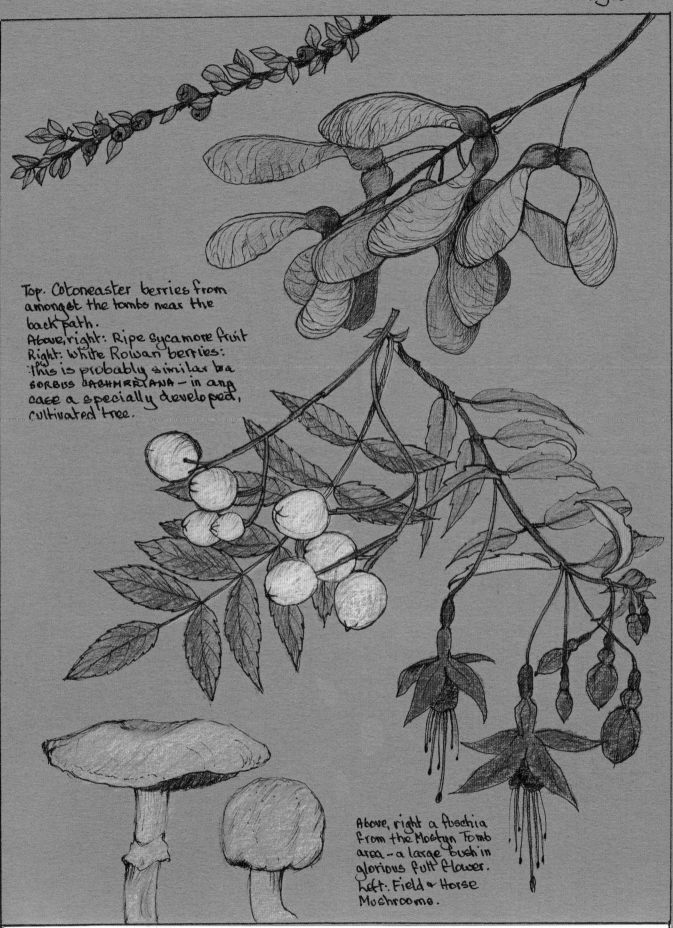

Top. Cotoneaster berries from amongst the tombs near the back path.
Above, right: Ripe Sycamore fruit
Right: White Rowan berries: This is probably similar to a SORBUS CASHMIRIANA — in any case a specially developed, cultivated tree.

Above, right a fuschia from the Mostyn Tomb area — a large bush in glorious full flower.
Left. Field & Horse Mushrooms.

Sunday, 29th.
A day of mixed cloud and some sunshine – warm. The churchyard has a mellow appearance with new grass growing through the strimmed debris. Interested to find someone had picked all the mushrooms in the back car park! Seed heads and fruit are the main items of interest.

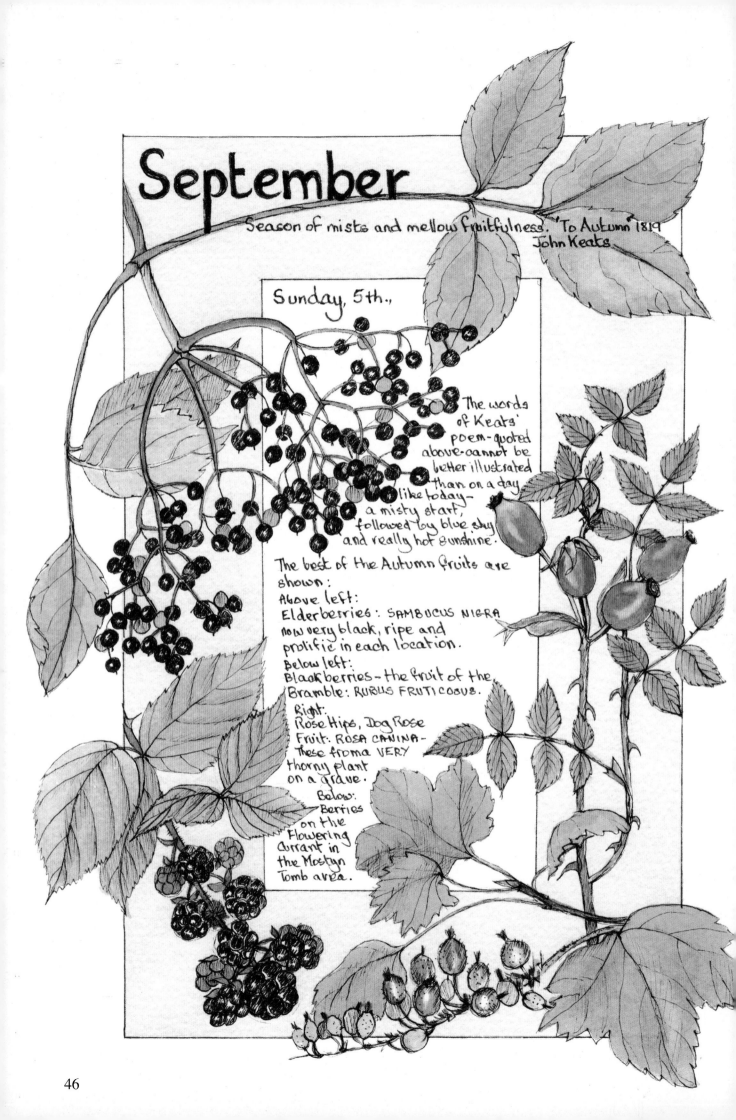

September

Season of mists and mellow fruitfulness. 'To Autumn' 1819
John Keats

Sunday, 5th.,

The words of Keats' poem - quoted above - cannot be better illustrated than on a day like today - a misty start, followed by blue sky and really hot sunshine.

The best of the Autumn fruits are shown:

Above left:
Elderberries: SAMBUCUS NIGRA now very black, ripe and prolific in each location.

Below left:
Blackberries - the fruit of the Bramble: RUBUS FRUTICOSUS.

Right:
Rose Hips, Dog Rose Fruit: ROSA CANINA - These from a VERY thorny plant on a grave.

Below:
Berries on the Flowering Currant in the Mostyn Tomb area.

Sunday, 12th.
Another beautiful Autumn day - still quite warm.

Ivy: HEDERA HELIX is now at its best. In the churchyard it is very prolific indeed and efforts are now being made to control it - at least over the gravestones.

Ivy flowers in October and fruits in the spring. SEE page 9.

Some branches never flower but, on other plants it seems that every branch flowers. The leaves are very variable in shape and are unlobed on flowering shoots.

Above right: An opulent flower display up the trunk of the big pine in the S.E. of the c'yard.

Variable lobed leaf shapes.

A flower bud + shiny unlobed leaves.

Round the page
Ivy on WALLS, TREES & GRAVESTONES

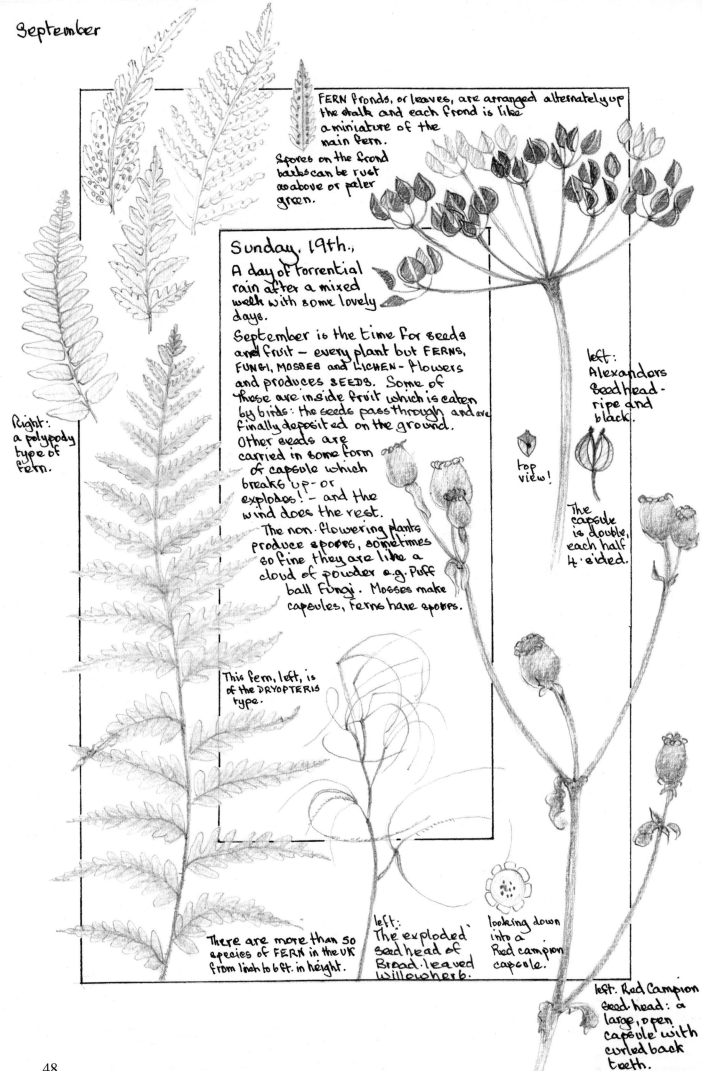

FERN fronds, or leaves, are arranged alternately up the stalk and each frond is like a miniature of the main fern.

Spores on the frond backs can be rust as above or paler green.

Right: a polypody type of fern.

Sunday. 19th.,

A day of torrential rain after a mixed week with some lovely days.

September is the time for seeds and fruit — every plant but FERNS, FUNGI, MOSSES and LICHEN - flowers and produces SEEDS. Some of those are inside fruit which is eaten by birds: the seeds pass through and are finally deposited on the ground. Other seeds are carried in some form of capsule which breaks up - or explodes! - and the wind does the rest.

The non-flowering plants produce spores, sometimes so fine they are like a cloud of powder e.g. Puff ball fungi. Mosses make capsules, ferns have spores.

This fern, left, is of the DRYOPTERIS type.

left: Alexandors Seed head - ripe and black.

top view!

The capsule is double, each half 4-sided.

There are more than 50 species of FERN in the UK from 1 inch to 6 ft. in height.

left: The "exploded" seed head of Broad-leaved Willowherb.

looking down into a Red campion capsule.

left: Red Campion Seed head: a large, open capsule with curled back teeth.

48

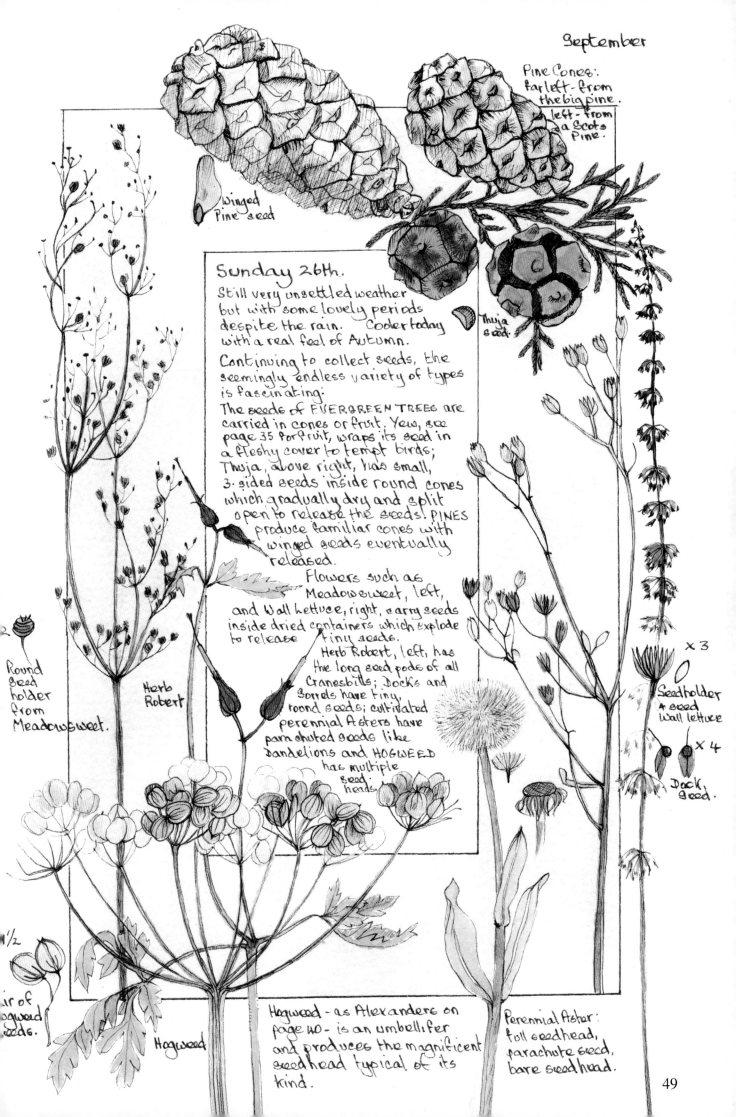

Pine Cones:
far left - from
the big pine.
left - from
a Scots
Pine.

Winged
Pine seed

Thuja
seed.

Sunday 26th.

Still very unsettled weather but with some lovely periods despite the rain. Cooler today with a real feel of Autumn.

Continuing to collect seeds, the seemingly endless variety of types is fascinating.

The seeds of EVERGREEN TREES are carried in cones or fruit. Yew, see page 35 for fruit, wraps its seed in a fleshy cover to tempt birds; Thuja, above right, has small, 3-sided seeds inside round cones which gradually dry and split open to release the seeds! PINES produce familiar cones with winged seeds eventually released.

Flowers such as Meadowsweet, left, and Wall Lettuce, right, carry seeds inside dried containers which explode to release tiny seeds.

Herb Robert, left, has the long seed pods of all Cranesbills; Docks and Sorrels have tiny, round seeds; cultivated perennial Asters have parachuted seeds like Dandelions and HOGWEED has multiple seed heads.

Round
seed
holder
from
Meadowsweet.

Herb
Robert

x 3

Seedholder
& seed
Wall lettuce.

x 4

Dock
seed.

½

pair of
Hogweed
seeds.

Hogweed

Hogweed - as Alexanders on page 40 - is an umbellifer and produces the magnificent seedhead typical of its kind.

Perennial Aster:
full seedhead,
parachute seed,
bare seedhead.

October

Sunday, 3rd.
A cool, Autumn day of heavy showers, winds & sunshine. Heavy rain during the week has drenched the churchyard which looks overgrown & green.

Sunday, 10th.
A very mild day - sunny at first with wind and light rain later. Autumn colours are showing on many plants but everywhere is still very green.

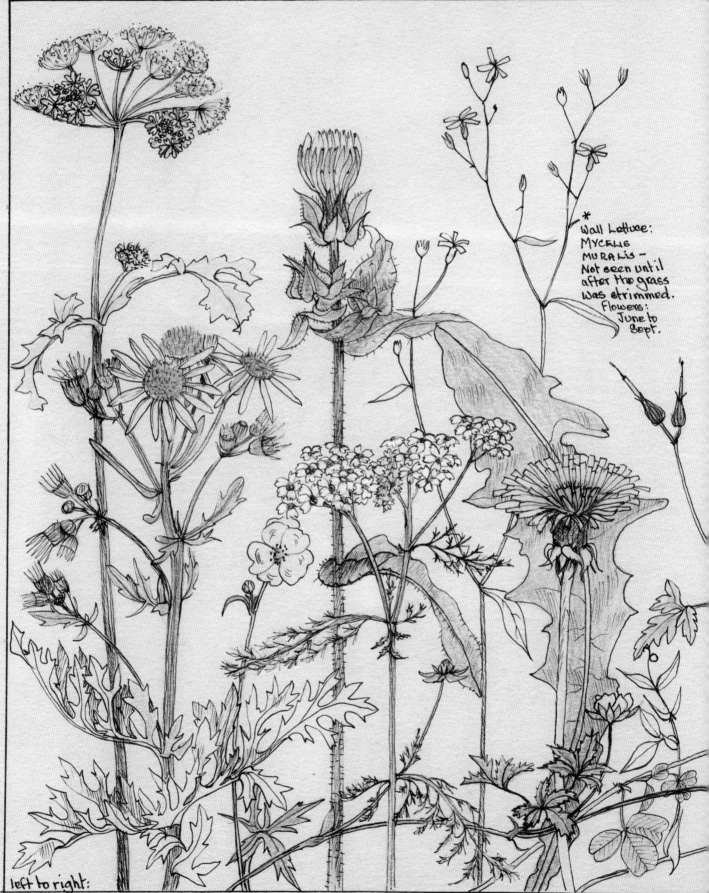

* Wall Lettuce: MYCELIS MURALIS - Not seen until after the grass was strimmed. Flowers: June to Sept.

left to right:

Hogweed. July: Ragwort. July: Buttercup. May: Prickly Sowthistle. April: Yarrow. August: Dandelion. April: Creeping
↳ More likely to be Bristly ox-tongue.

50

Sunday, 17th.
Another beautiful, sunny day, typical of the traditional St. Luke's Tide. Autumn in North Wales is a lovely season; frosts and fogs do not dominate the weather as in more Easterly regions.

Sunday, 24th.
A very wet day after a mild week. The paths of the church-yard are covered with wet, fallen leaves but the trees are becoming more colourful with soft, Autumn tints.

Sunday, 31st.
The clocks went back last night and its Hallowe'en today! Beautiful, sunny day but with a very strong wind blowing the leaves off the trees.

Autumn colours: A spray of Rosebay Willowherb behind, left to right: cultivated Cranesbill, Sycamore and Bindweed leaves.

Although the main flowering season for most wild plants is long since over by October, many have second flowerings and some eg. Herb Robert & Dandelions, only really stop when the frosts come.
This year, the grass of the churchyard is starred by late flowers, among them are the thirteen shown here.
The month when they were first seen and recorded is given beside each name.
Note that bulbs do not flower again – but violets and Primroses can be very early.

Cinquefoil: June: Herb Robert: June: Black Medick: May: Meadow Vetchling: June: Ox-eye Daisy: May: Red Clover: May.

51

November

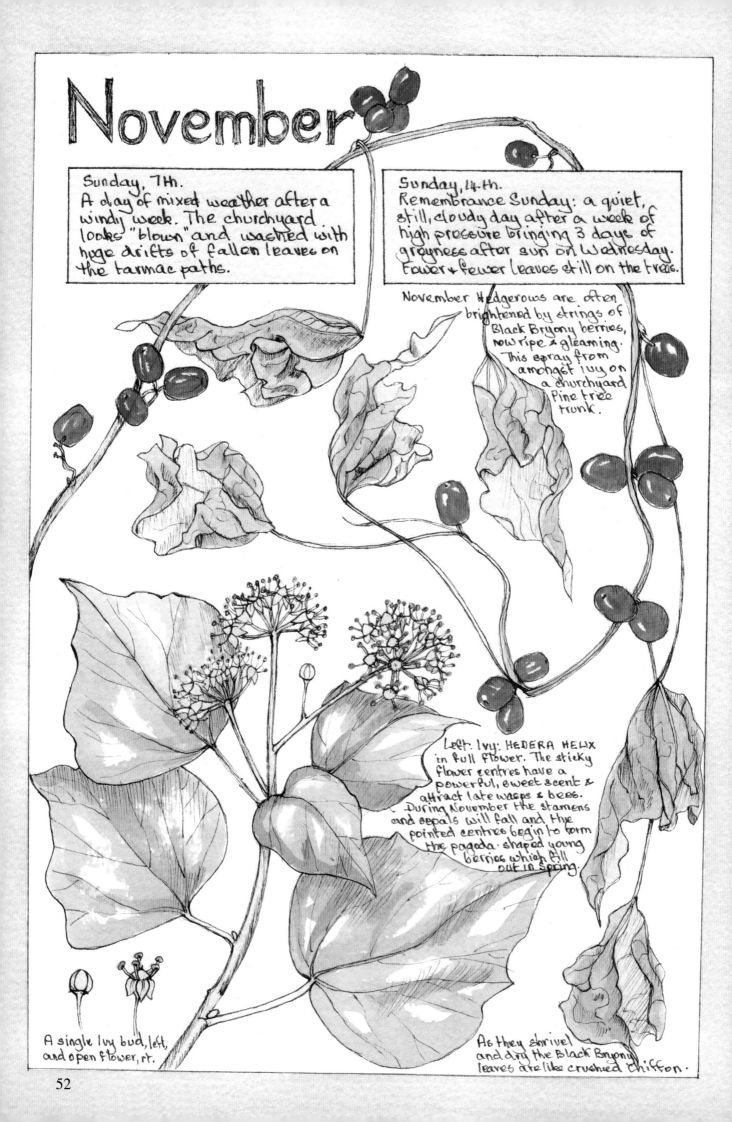

Sunday, 7th.
A day of mixed weather after a windy week. The churchyard looks "blown" and washed with huge drifts of fallen leaves on the tarmac paths.

Sunday, 14th.
Remembrance Sunday: a quiet, still, cloudy day after a week of high pressure bringing 3 days of greyness after sun on Wednesday. Fewer & fewer leaves still on the trees.

November Hedgerows are often brightened by strings of Black Bryony berries, now ripe & gleaming. This spray from amongst ivy on a churchyard Pine tree trunk.

Left: Ivy: HEDERA HELIX in full flower. The sticky flower centres have a powerful, sweet scent & attract late wasps & bees. During November the stamens and sepals will fall and the pointed centres begin to form the pagoda shaped young berries which fill out in Spring.

A single Ivy bud, left, and open flower, rt.

As they shrivel and dry the Black Bryony leaves are like crushed chiffon.

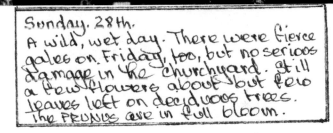

Right:
Two of the big
sycamores against
an Autumn blue sky:
one still with many
golden, turning leaves.

Sunday, 21st.
A crisp, cold, sunny day after a
wintry week with snow on the
high mountains. Various flowers
still blooming eg. Herb Robert, Daisies:
large & small and Ragwort.

Below:
The back gate path
towards the Mostyn
enclosure, thickly
carpeted with
fallen yew berries
which have been
prolific this year.

Sunday. 28th.
A wild, wet day. There were fierce
gales on Friday, too, but no serious
damage in the churchyard. Still
a few flowers about but few
leaves left on deciduous trees.
The PRUNUS are in full bloom.

Prunus:
beautifully coloured, delicate leaves.

Sycamore:
A tough, dried fallen leaf.

A misty view looking out towards Bryn Pydew.

Prunus: double-pink, in
winter flower.

The Angel (as left): a
long view in Autumn

Berries on English Yew.

Holly: berries - see page [...]

December

The Angel on the Hind tomb by the back path in the churchyard

Sunday, 5th.
A grey, wintry day with snow on the
higher mountains. The holly trees
in the churchyard look polished &
shiny. The two Prunus trees (see p. 4)
are in full flower and a few brave
daisies & the odd buttercup are in bloom.

Sunday, 12th.
A very wet, raw day after a week
of high winds and rain.
All the lower part of the churchyard
has now been strimmed and the
gravestones look bare!
The tree branches, all bare now on
the deciduous trees, like black lace.

Sunday, 19th.
A very cold, crisp, sunny day. This
past week has been wintry: snow
well down on the mountains and
overnight frosts. Everything is
drawn now in this diary and the
end of the work in sight!

Sunday, 26th.
The last entry!
A cold, grey day with snow low
down on the hills — after a
very wild week. Sheep in the
churchyard! Now for 2000 AD.

55

INDEX

The identification of wild plants is sometimes easy and, at other times, very difficult indeed. Efforts have been made to be as accurate as possible in this diary — but there are some guesses: educated, we hope! Mosses, Grasses and Fungi - specialist fields in their own right - have merely been touched upon, and some of the cultivated plants and trees have been identified by species only, not precise cultivars.

The English, or common, names are given in the full A-Z index, with the Latin names alongside. The latter are used universally, across all languages and are the most accurate method of description as English (and Welsh) names are often local or colloquial.

Some of the Latin terms are worth recognising as they provide helpful hints for identification.
Such as: MURALIS meaning "of walls",
ARVENSE meaning "of the field"
VULGARE/is - usual, common
PRATENSE/is - "of meadows".

BMM 27·12·99

A to Z : C indicates Cultivated plant; T indicates Tree or bush.

The gravestones in changing seasons:
above left: in February with snowdrops and,
above right: in March with daffodils.

In January, right, the whole area has a polished, tidy appearance, but in July, left+right above, luxuriant plant growth changes the aspects of granite + marble.

Meadowsweet & grasses, left, and sunlight on the back path, right.